Golf Injury
Handbook

Golf Injury Handbook

Professional Advice for Amateur Athletes

Allan M. Levy, M.D.
Mark L. Fuerst

John Wiley & Sons, Inc.

New York • Chichester • Weinheim • Brisbane • Singapore • Toronto

This book is printed on acid-free paper. ♾

The information contained in this book is not intended to serve as a replacement for professional medical advice. Any use of the information in this book is at the reader's discretion. The author and publisher specifically disclaim any and all liability arising directly or indirectly from the use or application of any information contained in this book. A health care professional should be consulted regarding your specific situation.

Library of Congress Cataloging-in-Publication Data:

Levy, Allan M.
    Golf injury handbook : professional advice for amateur athletes /
Allan M. Levy, Mark L. Fuerst.
        p. cm.
    Includes index.
    ISBN 0-471-24853-3 (pbk. : alk. paper)
    1. Golf injuries. I. Fuerst, Mark. II. Title.
RC1220.G64L48   1999
617.1'027—dc21   98-24885

Printed in the United States of America

10 9 8 7 6 5 4 3 2 1

Contents

Exercises

Foreword

As a professional instructor and golf coach to top tour players as well as numerous weekend golfers, I must stay on the cutting edge of my sport. It's either that or watch the world pass me by.

There are so many new ideas and so much general information regarding every aspect of the game, it is hard to keep up. Yet, of course, it is something I love to do.

The centerpiece of my golf-school teaching system is the "25 percent theory." That simply means our instructors divide golf into four equal parts: the long game, the short game, the mental game, and the management game. These four basic areas make up the golfer's talent profile. What the golfer needs to improve will always fall into one of these four categories. The job of our teachers is to accurately diagnose what each golfer needs to work on first, and then develop an improvement plan.

As teaching and coaching golf have become more and more refined, the area of golf management has been taken much more seriously. I've seen a huge change in just the last ten years. To me, the management game means how you manage your golf strengths and weaknesses. It includes how you manage your life. Depending upon how much you want to improve and how dedicated you are, your off-course management skills become more important.

Today, all PGA Tour players consider physical conditioning and stretching as absolute fundamentals to success. Many of golf's greatest players have full-time trainers or have very detailed training programs.

If you are not training like an athlete, you are losing tremendous ground and you simply will not make it in today's ultramodern, high-tech world.

I've noticed that many average golfers attending our schools are seeking our advice on flexibility and strength training. They have become aware that without good range of motion, they will never hit the ball as they had hoped.

So getting the right information from the huge number of available sources is key. Just as in golf instruction, there is an information overload, with a high percentage of that information being very weak and sometimes highly detrimental.

In *Golf Injury Handbook*, you will get great information from Dr. Allan Levy and Mark Fuerst. These two top professionals can give you cutting-edge information in the field of sports medicine. I'm sure that following their advice will allow you to do more with the golf club and help you reach your true golf potential—and have much more fun playing the game.

The one key word that describes every successful person I've ever met is *preparation.* This book will help you prepare for a wide variety of potential problems. It includes all kinds of advice and ideas on preventing problems before they happen, as well as fixing physical problems that you may already have.

Prepare to succeed in golf by examining the management department of your golf life. This book will definitely help you get ready to play your best golf.

Best of luck,
Jim McLean

Acknowledgments

We would like to thank the many people who helped make this book possible:

John "Mother" Dunn, strength coach of the New York Giants, for his help with the conditioning programs.

John Mancuso, video director of the Giants, for his help in putting the exercise illustrations together.

Jon Eisen and the members of South Fork Country Club, who provided guidance, anecdotal material, and a great place to play.

Kevin Smith and his staff at Montauk Downs State Park for direction and consultation and for helping me (MLF) begin to find my game.

Our agent, Faith Hamlin, of Sanford J. Greenburger Associates, Inc., for continuing to guide us in spreading the word.

Judith McCarthy and the staff at John Wiley for editorial and production quality, and Jackie Aher for her skillful illustrations.

To my wife, Gail, who not only put up with my extra hours putting this down on paper, but then did all of my typing, copying, and faxing as well (AML).

To my wife, Margie, for her enduring support during the long hours of writing and organizing the manuscript. I only wish I had a game as good as hers (MLF).

Golf Injury
Handbook

Introduction

Slipped discs, tendinitis, aching shoulders, pulled muscles, inflamed rotator cuffs. Injuries from a pickup football game? Try a round of golf.

Getting injured playing golf is par for the course. More than half of golfers below age 50, and 65 percent of golfers over age 50, have suffered some type of injury while golfing. After a round of golf, three out of four players complain of lower back pain because swinging a club makes them twist unnaturally, over and over again. It's estimated that the average golfer takes 300 swings (including practice swings) during a round.

Golf is surprisingly rigorous. While it won't do much to improve conditioning, particularly if you ride a cart, golfers do need to be in shape to play, especially to play well. A seemingly gentle recreation, golf can really beat up the body. Professionals generate more than enough torque during the swing to rupture discs in the lower portion of the spine. Amateurs have it even worse because they often do not use their hips properly, which would take some stress off the back.

As golf has become more popular, I have seen more hackers hobble into my sports medicine practice. A little education about the stresses of golf on the body helps them avoid common injuries and recover from various aches and pains. Many of these injuries can be prevented if golfers would pay attention to basic fitness and correct form.

To help prevent golfing injuries, I have developed a program to help golfers improve their performance. The program involves a basic, at-home fitness routine consisting of exercises to lengthen and strengthen muscles pertinent to golf.

Golfers who increase flexibility and strengthen muscles can prevent injuries and improve their scores. Many amateur golfers can't even get into the proper position to swing because they are not flexible enough. If they become more flexible, they will have a smoother swing. Getting into shape and strengthening the wrist, the elbow, the shoulders, and the stomach muscles also helps. Good shape and good form mean fewer injuries.

This book outlines a series of simple flexibility and strengthening exercises that can be done before and even during a round. The idea is not to turn golfers into weight lifters or marathoners. It's to show them a few things that might prevent injuries and, in the long run, help them play better golf.

HOW TO USE THIS BOOK

In Part One, I take you through the essential elements of a proper workout to lower your score. That includes warm-up and stretching, conditioning, and strength training. I also provide sound advice on what foods to eat before, during, and after a round for peak performance.

The stretching program will increase your flexibility. Flexibility is particularly important for the middle-aged golfer who tries to swing a club the first nice spring weekend. Returning to action after a long layoff puts you at high risk of an injury. Overstretching a joint or muscle may result in a sprain or muscle pull, causing many miserable Mondays after a weekend of golf.

The strength training program will help you build muscles throughout the body. Golfers have traditionally avoided weight training because they think it bulks them up and reduces their flexibility. Every golfer would like to hit the ball farther, and proper strength training can help you do that without compromising flexibility.

In Part Two, I focus on common concerns and fundamental precautions for golfers regarding who gets injured, including a rehabilitation timetable, and medical problems they may face. I also review golf gadgets being marketed to enhance your health and to improve strength and flexibility.

Part Three provides a complete guide to golf injuries, organized by area of the body, from head to toe. You will learn how to recognize and treat injuries to each body part and determine when it's safe to play again. You'll also discover how to prevent reinjury using specific exercises. I give practical advice, not just theoretical applications. For example, to strengthen your wrists, you can squeeze a soft rubber ball bought from a five-and-dime store instead of expensive hand putty from a surgical supply house.

Any amateur can learn the rehabilitation techniques that professional golfers use. Double-digit handicappers may not have the time to devote to rehabilitating themselves and working on their games as pros do, but the methods are the same. It's just a matter of degree.

Next to each condition in Part Three you'll find a symbol. These symbols help you understand whether you can begin to self-treat the condition or whether you must see a doctor or go for emergency treatment. The conditions are coded in the following way:

The first-aid symbol indicates that you may be able to treat the condition on your own initially with some basic first aid, though you may have to see a doctor later. Most golf injuries fall into this category—for example, a strained lower back muscle.

This symbol means that you need to see a doctor directly for treatment, even though the injury may seem to be minor and not that painful, such as elbow pain after you hit into the ground. Rest and ice alone won't relieve the pain of torn muscle or tendon fibers. You need to see a doctor for special treatment.

This symbol indicates an emergency situation—a condition such as getting hit on the head with a golf ball that needs immediate medical treatment in a hospital or an emergency care facility.

Part Four offers additional information on special concerns for senior, female, and disabled golfers, including special tips on how they can improve their games.

Part One

Preparing to Play

Fit for Golf

Eat to Compete

1

Fit for Golf

Whether professionals or weed whackers, all golfers should condition and prepare themselves to play. Golf is a game that involves almost every body part. Golfers who leave one part out will see it in their games and feel it the next day.

Most golfers lack a regular golf-related fitness routine. As a round of golf progresses, fatigue sets in and the golfer's game and form deteriorate, increasing the chance of injury. The repercussions include the inevitable poor performance, decreased playing time, increased incidence of injury, and taking time off from the game completely to recover. And golf injuries are on the rise. Because of the sport's growing popularity, golf injuries rose 13 percent from 1990 to 1995, according to the Consumer Product Safety Commission.

Because many players have age-related or pre-existing physical conditions, a general conditioning program and pre-game warm-up are essential to prevent injuries. The good news is that many injuries can be prevented if you pay attention to basic fitness and correct form. When you work the muscles pertinent to golf, you'll become stronger and more flexible, and you can hit the ball farther and more consistently. An at-home program of stretching and strengthening exercises a few days a week is all it takes.

Fortunately, golfers are a unique breed and will do almost anything to improve their games. People who ordinarily would never think of strength training will do it if it adds a few yards to their drives.

Coupling strength and flexibility training can boost your fitness and performance.

WARM UP TO AVOID COLD GOLF

A pro football player or a mile runner would never dream of performing without first warming up. Yet most golfers rush out to the links Saturday morning, lace on their shoes, hustle to the first tee, and begin hitting away without the slightest warm-up or stretching. Golf makes bona fide athletic demands on the body. Without a proper warm-up before playing a round or practicing, you are bound to become injured.

How do you go about warming up? Before playing, do light calisthenics (arm circles, leg kicks, simulated swings without a club), take a brisk walk, jog lightly, ride a stationary bicycle in the locker room, or do any other easy exercise gradually until you get the heart pumping. This increases blood flow to the muscles. The goal is to raise the body's temperature by about 2°F, which leads to warm, loose muscles and joints.

How do you know when your body temperature has gone up? Luckily, most recreational athletes don't need to carry a thermometer. The body has its own natural thermometer: when you break into a sweat, your body temperature has been elevated by about 2°F.

Warming up systematically can help you achieve peak performance. Try to get to the course about an hour before your tee time so you don't have to rush. After warming up your muscles for 5 to 10 minutes, loosen up with long, slow swings with two clubs at once or with a weighted club. Or add a weight donut (originally designed for on-deck batters in baseball) to the end of a club.

When you are finally ready to hit a few practice shots, find a comfortable tempo and balance. Start with wedges and short irons, then progress to middle irons and woods. Shorter clubs put less stress on your body, so wait until your muscles are completely loose before hitting the driver.

You only need to hit about 40 full shots before going out to play. Most professionals hit a few shots with each of about a half dozen clubs. For example, you may want to hit only your odd-numbered irons and two woods. The next time you warm up before playing, hit only your even-numbered irons and two woods. Now you can hit some chips, roll some putts to gauge the speed of the green, and gain the confidence you need to shoot the lowest score possible.

CONDITIONING

Golf is not only fun, it's good for you. Golf is a lifelong sport that's excellent for weight control because it's an activity that is low in intensity but long in duration. A round of golf, walking and pulling clubs for 18 holes, burns almost 1,000 calories for an average 150-pound man, which is the equivalent of running 6 miles. Walk the course (which is like a 5-mile hike over hilly terrain) and carry your bag, and you may burn up to 2,000 calories.

Good conditioning can prevent golf injuries and allow golfers to improve their skills. Cardiovascular conditioning, or heart health, is important to be able to walk the full course. In fact, walking and a healthy heart go hand in hand. Studies show that golfers who walk 18 holes three times a week and carry their bags can raise the level of "good," high-density lipoprotein (HDL) cholesterol.

If you can't walk the whole course, try to walk between two fairway shots as a starter. Or have your partner drop you off the cart 50 yards in front of your ball. You will be surprised how fast your body responds. Walking keeps your muscles warm for the next shot, gets the blood flowing, and steadies your breathing. Walking also helps you to focus on the upcoming shot so you will be both physically and mentally prepared by the time you reach your ball.

Walking also helps you regain composure after a bad shot. Take some deep breaths as you approach the ball and get ready to hit the next shot. Also, try walking onto the green from the front, even if the cart is parked to the side. This gives a good perspective on the shape and contour of the green and helps in reading putts.

Good physical conditioning also pays off on the course. Coming down the wire, if you are physically fit, you are less likely to get shaky hands and miss a putt. Most golfers' blood pressure rises when they walk into a sand trap. If you are cardiovascularly fit, you will be better prepared, more calm and focused to hit the shot, and more likely to get up and down.

FLEXIBILITY

A full range of motion is the key to golf. To have a good swing, you need to take a full turn. Typically, a golfer's swing becomes more restricted with increasing pressure to perform, as well as with advancing age. A golfer who is more flexible and has greater mobility in the joints and muscles will have a more fluid, less-restricted swing.

Without flexibility, the golfer's body is subject to abnormal stresses that can lead to injury. However, spending just a little time stretching regularly will give you an edge over your golfing buddies and consistently shave a few strokes off your scores. It also helps insulate you from injury. A little stretching may end up saving you months of discomfort.

A recent study of 1,000 golfers at the PGA National Resort & Spa in Florida found that men and women with higher flexibility tend to be better golfers. Increasing overall flexibility in the muscle groups used in golf will maximize swinging power and clubhead speed, improve control, and help reduce the risk of injury.

Most men need more flexibility than strength work (the opposite is generally true of women). Because of all the hyper-rotation and side-to-side bending, golf exercises that emphasize the rotary movements of the trunk and forearms are important. The legs are the foundation of the swing and are tied in to the twisting torso, and must be supple as well as strong.

Yoga, including newer variations such as fitness yoga and power yoga, is another form of flexibility training that helps golfers, particularly with movements that promote spine agility and balance. Yoga is a good way to add flexibility, stamina, and a sense of peace. Yoga lengthens and strengthens the muscles while reinforcing the connection between the mind and the body.

Yoga classes can be found at special studios or health clubs across the country. Videotapes for beginners to those more advanced are also available. One attraction is that you can do yoga in your living room, back porch, or any quiet place. You can also do yoga year-round to maintain your flexibility.

The following illustrated head-to-toe stretching program is designed specifically for golfers. The program contains two parts. The first part includes stretches to be done as part of your regular exercise routine off the course for the hamstrings, calves, Achilles tendons, hips, trunk and lower back, shoulder, elbows, and neck. The second part contains a pre-round stretching program to be done before playing or practicing.

As with any stretching program, first warm up for 5 to 10 minutes to get your muscles loose and limber by jogging in place or doing light calisthenics. Then you can start your stretching program before hitting balls.

FLEXIBILITY OFF THE COURSE

Hamstring Stretches

Hurdler Stretch (Sitting)

Sit with your right leg extended and your left foot on the inside of your right knee. Lean forward and grasp your right foot with both hands. Hold for 20 seconds. Repeat with the left leg extended.

Hurdler Stretch (Standing)

While standing, put one foot on the seat or the back of a chair in front of you, depending on your flexibility. Now bend your forehead forward and try to touch your knee. Hold the stretch for 15 to 20 seconds. Repeat three times. Repeat with the other leg.

Calf and Achilles Stretches

Wall Push-Up

Place one foot as far away from a wall as you can and still keep your rear heel flat on the ground and the other leg a few inches from the wall. Bending your elbows, lean into the wall and support yourself with your hands, but don't let your rear heel come off the ground. Hold the stretch for 15 to 20 seconds, then bend the knee towards the wall, again keeping your rear heel on the floor. You will feel the stretch higher in your calf. Hold for 15 to 20 seconds. Repeat three times.

Heel Drop

Stand with your forefeet on a raised surface, as if you were going to do a back dive off a diving board. Let your weight take your heels down below the level of the surface so that the back of your calf is stretched. Hold for 15 to 20 seconds and come back up. Repeat until your calf is fully fatigued.

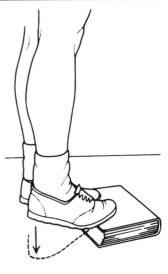

Hip Stretches

Hip Flexors (Quadriceps) Stretch

Stand next to a wall and pull the foot of one leg toward the buttocks with your hand. Balance yourself against the wall with your other hand and attempt to arch your back. Hold for 15 to 20 seconds and then relax. Repeat five times.

Hip Extension

Lie on your back on a table with one leg hanging over the side. Gently lower the leg from the hip toward the floor. When you feel the stretch in your hip, hold for 15 seconds. If possible, have a partner push on your knee to increase the stretch. Return your leg to table height and repeat the stretch five times. Add stretches two at a time as this becomes easier.

Lunge Stretch

Stand with your hands at your side and then lunge forward with your left leg until your foot is below your knee. Support yourself with your hands and hold for 20 seconds. Repeat on the opposite side. Do three repetitions on each side.

Lotus Stretch

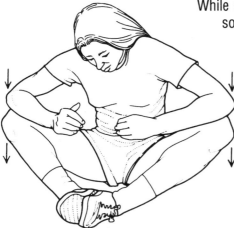

While sitting down, bend your knees so that the soles of your feet are touching each other. Now put your elbows on your knees and gradually push them outward. Hold for 20 to 30 seconds. Repeat three times.

Knee-over-Leg Stretch (Iliotibial Band Stretch)

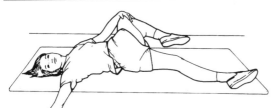

While lying flat on your back, bend your right leg and bring it across your body to the left side. Hold the right knee down with the left hand and lean your shoulders and head back to the right. Hold for 20 seconds and then repeat on the other side. Do three repetitions on each side.

Side Saddle Stretch

Stand with your legs 3 feet apart, and gradually bend one knee and lean your body toward that side. Keep your trunk straight. Hold the stretch for 20 to 30 seconds. Repeat three times.

Trunk and Lower Back Stretches

Forehead-to-Knee Stretch

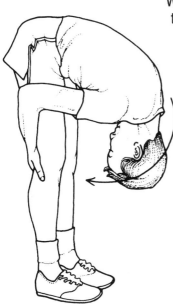

While standing, grab your knees and try to touch your forehead to your knees. Hold for 15 to 20 seconds. Start with three repetitions and then increase gradually by one every other day until you reach 12 repetitions.

Toe Touch with Rotation

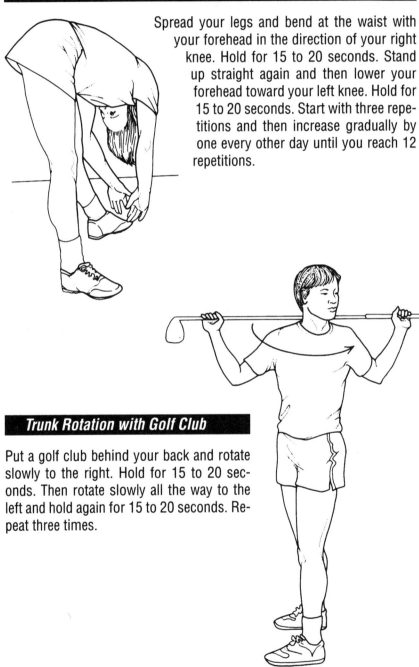

Spread your legs and bend at the waist with your forehead in the direction of your right knee. Hold for 15 to 20 seconds. Stand up straight again and then lower your forehead toward your left knee. Hold for 15 to 20 seconds. Start with three repetitions and then increase gradually by one every other day until you reach 12 repetitions.

Trunk Rotation with Golf Club

Put a golf club behind your back and rotate slowly to the right. Hold for 15 to 20 seconds. Then rotate slowly all the way to the left and hold again for 15 to 20 seconds. Repeat three times.

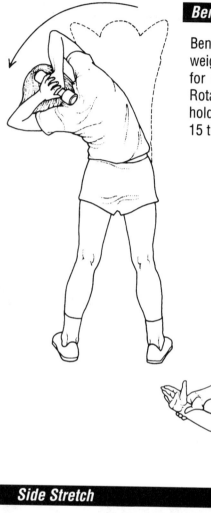

Bent-Waist Rotation

Bend at the waist and hold a small weight (10 pounds for men, 5 pounds for women) at the back of your neck. Rotate from side to side, each time holding at the extreme of the stretch for 15 to 20 seconds. Do five repetitions.

Side Stretch

Stand with your hands over your head. Grasp your right wrist with your left hand and lean to the right. Hold for 20 seconds, and then switch sides and repeat. Do three repetitions.

Extension Stretch

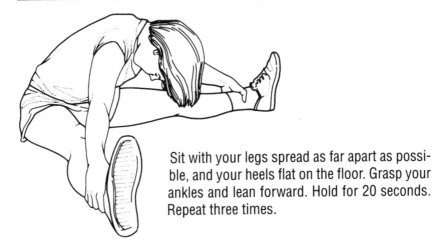

Sit with your legs spread as far apart as possible, and your heels flat on the floor. Grasp your ankles and lean forward. Hold for 20 seconds. Repeat three times.

"V" Stretch

Sit with your legs spread in a "V" position, heels on the floor. Lean to one side and grasp your ankle or foot. Hold for 20 seconds and then grasp the other ankle or foot for 20 more seconds. Repeat three times.

Forward Stretch

Sit with your legs together and extended straight out. Lean forward at the waist and grasp your ankles or feet. Hold for 20 seconds. Repeat three times.

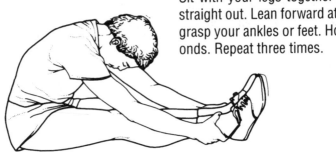

Knee Pull

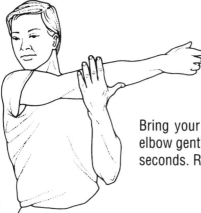

Lie flat on your back and grasp one knee with interlaced fingers. Keeping your back flat, pull your knee toward your chest and hold for 20 seconds. Switch to the other knee and repeat the stretch. Do three repetitions.

Shoulder Stretches

Arm across Chest

Bring your arm across your chest and pull the elbow gently with the opposite hand. Hold for 20 seconds. Repeat three times.

Shoulder Rotation

Face a doorway or post, grasp the doorway or post, and rotate your body away from the doorway or post to stretch the front of the shoulder. Hold for 20 seconds. Repeat three times.

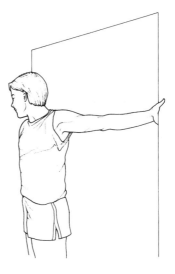

Arm Overhead

Bring your arm up over your head and pull the elbow gently with the opposite hand. Hold for 20 seconds. Repeat on the opposite side. Do three repetitions.

Elbow Stretches

Palm Up

Extend your arm straight out, parallel to the floor with the elbow locked, palm facing up. With your other hand, push the palm and fingers of the extended hand toward the floor. Hold for 15 to 20 seconds. Repeat three times.

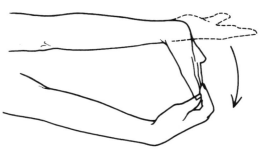

Palm Down

Extend your arm straight out, parallel to the floor with the elbow locked, palm facing down. Push the top of your hand and fingers of the extended hand down toward the floor with the other hand. Hold for 15 to 20 seconds. Repeat three times.

Neck Stretches

Chin Drop

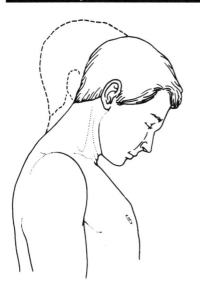

Gently drop your chin to your chest. Now move your chin in a semicircle from shoulder to shoulder five times.

Trapezius Stretch

Sit in a chair and hold onto the seat with one hand. Bend your head and trunk to the opposite side and hold for 15 to 20 seconds. Do three repetitions. Repeat on the other side.

PRE-ROUND STRETCHING

A pre-round stretching program is the best way to avoid a traumatic muscle pull. Most golfers, if they do stretch, tend to overstretch their muscles before a round. There is a right way and a wrong way to stretch before hitting a golf ball. The way most golfers stretch their backs is more destructive than helpful. Typically, a golfer puts a club behind the back and rotates back and forth rapidly. You would be better off not stretching at all. Every time you rotate during this ballistic type of stretch, receptors fire and shorten the muscle, which is the opposite of what you want.

The following exercises are designed to help you stretch correctly and, as a result, improve your performance on the course. If you arrive at the course just before your tee time, warm up your muscles rather than stretch them. A warm, loose muscle will stretch itself out during practice swings. You are better off jogging in place or doing jumping jacks than trying to stretch cold muscles. Of course, the best thing is to get to the course in time to both warm up and stretch your muscles.

Unfortunately, most golfers don't warm up at all. Golfers who don't stretch or work out with weights are notorious for not loosening up before going out to play. Most professional golfers, on the other hand, take at least 45 minutes to warm up and stretch before they hit any balls.

Hamstrings and Calves

Hurdler Stretch (Standing)   *See page 11.*
Wall Push-Up   *See page 12.*

Hips

Hip Flexors (Quadriceps) Stretch   *See page 13.*
Side Saddle Stretch   *See page 15.*

Trunk and Lower Back

Forehead-to-Knee Stretch   *See page 15.*
Toe Touch with Rotation   *See page 16.*
Trunk Rotation with Golf Club   *See page 16.*
Side Stretch   *See page 17.*

Shoulders

Arm across Chest   *See page 19.*
Shoulder Rotation   *See page 19.*
Arm Overhead   *See page 20.*

Elbows

Elbow Stretch (Palm Up)   *See page 20.*
Elbow Stretch (Palm Down)   *See page 20.*

STRENGTHEN YOURSELF AND YOUR GAME

Hitting a golf ball consistently and effectively for 18 holes requires coordinated muscular control, strength, and stamina. At least 32 major muscles are involved in a full golf swing. These muscles must be used in the proper sequence to achieve a fluid, effective swing.

Strength is just as important in golf as accuracy. Not only will it enable you to hit the ball farther, but it will cut down on the number of injuries you suffer.

While golf is not a game of strength, strength will allow a golfer to hit with more consistent, explosive power over extended periods. A recent study shows that golfers who did 30 minutes of total body strength training three times a week for eight weeks increased their swing speed by 5 miles per hour, resulting in longer drives.

Anyone can add muscles and, as a result, add yards to his or her shots. The average driving distance on the PGA Tour has risen by almost 13 yards to nearly 270 yards since 1980, which is probably due to a combination of titanium drivers and more players pumping more iron in the gym. In general, golfers should not be interested in bulking up by spending hours in the gym lifting heavy weights. Instead, do a high number of repetitions with light weights, which will not bulk up your muscles or ruin your touch.

Weight machines in the gym may be easier to work with, but they limit the direction in which force can be applied to your muscles. Free weights, such as dumbbells and barbells, allow you to vary the path of motion of the weight and thus more easily adjust to strength differences between the two sides of your body.

Strengthening the legs is most important. The power of the golf swing comes from the legs. Taller players therefore have a mechanical advantage over smaller players. But even smaller players can be giant killers—just look at Justin Leonard, Gary Player, and the immortal Ben Hogan. They improved their strength and kept up with the Big Hitters.

Many golfers have bad backs. Swinging a club can put stress on your back equal to eight times your body weight. Also, the jolting contact of the club against the ground can send tremors up your spine. And bouncing around bent over the wheel of a golf cart puts unnecessary stress on your back muscles.

If you use your large trunk muscles when hitting the ball, you can generate much more power than you can with the smaller muscles of the arms and shoulders. Tiger Woods's legendary swing is due less to his wiry arms than to his strong, flexible trunk, which allows him to gracefully coil and uncoil his body, unleashing power that drives the ball more than 300 yards down the fairway. So I have included several trunk-strengthening exercises.

To generate power as you pull the club through the swing, you need strong shoulders. The forearms and wrists are particularly important in golf because they are used to give the ball added impetus. They also control the path of the swing and the accuracy of the shot. If you become stronger, you don't have to swing the club as hard or grip it as tightly.

STRENGTHENING EXERCISES

The following strengthening exercises should be done at least three times a week in the off-season. When you are playing frequently, reduce the frequency and number of repetitions of each exercise. However, strictly weekend golfers should maintain the same number of repetitions and do the entire program twice a week to maintain their strength.

If you do nothing else, at least do the trunk rotation and the forearm and wrist exercises. These exercises done year-round are the best way to stay strong during the off-season.

Lower Back and Lower Abdomen

Abdominal Bracing

Lie flat on your back with your knees bent and feet flat on the floor. Contract your abdominal muscles and pull one leg toward your chest. Now straighten the leg from the knee joint without lifting or rotating the hips. Return your leg to the starting position, pause, and lift your other leg in a similar motion. Do three sets of 10 repetitions.

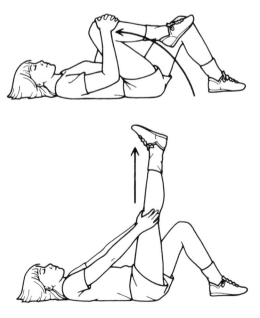

Bridging

Lie flat on your back with your knees bent and feet flat on the floor. Contract your abdominal muscles and, using your buttock muscles, slowly rise off the floor without bending your lower back. Keep your pelvis elevated 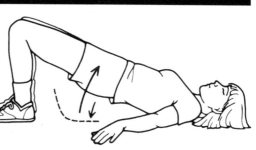 by using your abdominal and buttock muscles. Hold for one second, then return to the starting position. Do three sets of 10 repetitions.

Quadruped Leg Press

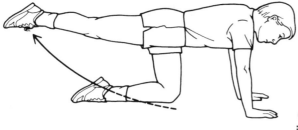 Kneel on all fours with your back flat. Contract your abdominal muscles, and slowly raise and straighten one leg by tightening the buttock and hamstring muscles. Concentrate on keeping your trunk stabilized while you move your leg. Do 10 repetitions with one leg, then 10 more with the other leg. Repeat three times.

Abdominal Crunch

Lie flat on your back with your knees bent and feet flat on the floor, with your hands clasped behind your head. Use your abdominal muscles to raise your upper back off the floor. Raise only the shoulder blades off the floor. Hold for 5 seconds, then return to the starting position. Keep your feet flat on the floor and move in a steady, smooth motion. Do three sets of 10 repetitions.

Pelvic Tilt

While lying on your back with knees bent and feet flat on the floor, relax the back muscles and tighten your abdominal and buttock muscles to press your back flat against the floor. This will tilt your pelvis forward. Hold for 5 seconds. Do three sets of 10 repetitions.

Back Extension

Lie flat on your stomach with your hands clasped behind your head. Slowly raise your head and shoulders off the floor while arching your back. If you can't do this, support part of your weight with your hands and elbows. Hold for 5 seconds. Do three repetitions and work your way up to one set of 10 repetitions.

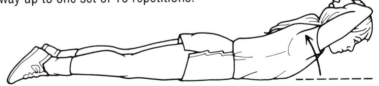

Hamstrings

Leg Curls

Lie face down on a bench with your head over the edge. Hold the bottom of the bench for support. Begin with your right leg straight and left leg bent at the knee, foot flexed. Lift the weight

with your left thigh up as high as possible while keeping your right foot on the bench. Pause at the top and then lower your leg. Do three sets of 10 repetitions. Repeat with the other leg.

Quadriceps

Leg Extension

Sit on a bench or leg extension machine with your legs at a 90° angle and feet flexed (soles parallel to the floor). Hold the bottom of the bench for support and rapidly lift the weight with one leg to full extension (toes pointing up). Hold for 3 seconds and slowly bring your leg back down. Do three sets of 10 repetitions.

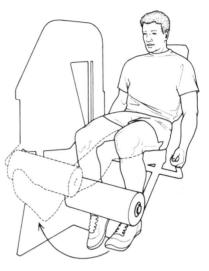

90-90 Wall Sitting

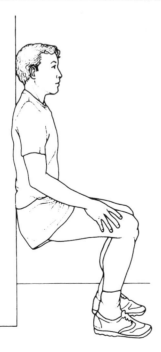

Put your back against a wall, with your knees bent as if you were sitting in a chair. Both your knees and hips should be at 90° angles. (In effect, you are sitting on air against a wall.) Maintain this position until your quadriceps burn and begin to give out. (This time may range from 30 seconds when you are starting out to 5 to 10 minutes when your legs are strong.) Repeat three times during the day.

Calves

Toe Raise

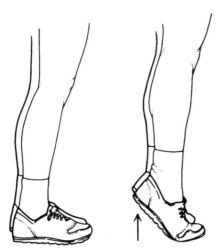

Stand on your toes for 10 seconds and then come down flat on the floor. Repeat until you feel real fatigue in your calf muscles.

As the calf muscles begin to strengthen, you can put all of your weight on one leg and keep the other leg off the floor. Then you can hold dumbbells or a barbell to increase your body weight. Do all of the lifting with one leg, using the other leg for balance, then switch legs.

Shoulder

For all of the shoulder exercises, keep the amount of weight below 15 pounds to make sure only the shoulder muscles are being used, not the back and arm muscles. Do the following exercises until fatigue sets in or for 50 repetitions once a day.

Front Lift (Palm Down)

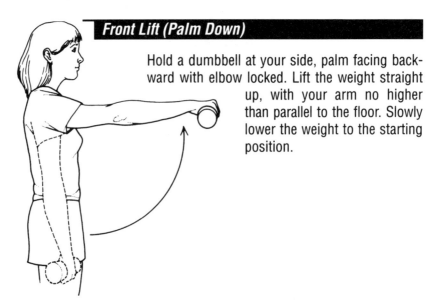

Hold a dumbbell at your side, palm facing backward with elbow locked. Lift the weight straight up, with your arm no higher than parallel to the floor. Slowly lower the weight to the starting position.

Front Lift (Palm Up)

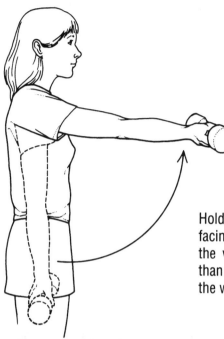

Hold a dumbbell at your side, palm facing forward with elbow locked. Lift the weight straight up, but no more than parallel to the floor. Slowly lower the weight to the starting position.

Lateral Lift

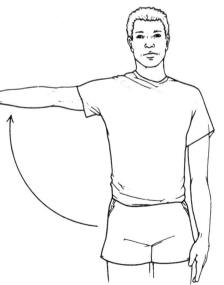

Hold a dumbbell at your side, palm facing the body. Lift the weight to the side, with your arm no higher than parallel to the floor. Slowly lower the weight to the starting position.

Bent-Over Lateral Lift

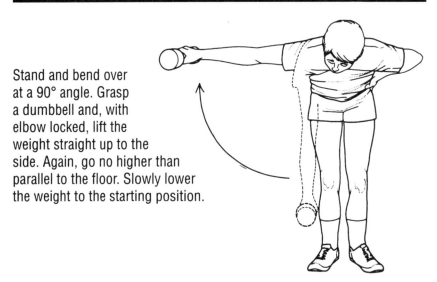

Stand and bend over at a 90° angle. Grasp a dumbbell and, with elbow locked, lift the weight straight up to the side. Again, go no higher than parallel to the floor. Slowly lower the weight to the starting position.

Bent-Over Chest Lift

Stand and bend over at a 90° angle. Grasp a dumbbell and, with elbow locked, lift the weight across your chest. Slowly lower the weight to the starting position.

Elbow

For these elbow exercises, you will need a small dumbbell—5 pounds for men, 2.5 pounds for women. Gradually increase the weight as your strength improves.

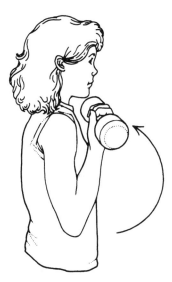

Arm Curl

Hold a dumbbell with your palm facing forward and your hand at your side. Bend your elbow and lift the weight to your shoulder. Slowly lower the weight to the starting position. Do 50 repetitions or until fatigue sets in.

Reverse Arm Curl

Hold a dumbbell with your palm facing backward and your hand at your side. Bend your elbow and lift the weight to your shoulder. Slowly lower the weight to the starting position. Do 50 repetitions or until muscle exhaustion results.

Wrist Curl

Hold a dumbbell with your arm down by your side and your elbow locked. With your palm facing forward, flex the wrist forward and then let it back down. Repeat 50 times or until the muscle is exhausted.

Reverse Wrist Curl

Put your arm down by your side and turn your hand so that the palm faces backward. Holding a dumbbell, flex the wrist forward as far as it will go and then let it down. Repeat 50 times or to the point of muscle exhaustion.

Unbalanced Wrist Rotation

With your arm extended outward, hold the dumbbell by one knob so that the shaft and the other knob comes out on the thumb side of your hand. Now rotate your wrist so that the other knob rotates to the left, then all the way to the right, and then back to center again. Do 50 complete left-to-right rotations or repeat until muscle exhaustion sets in.

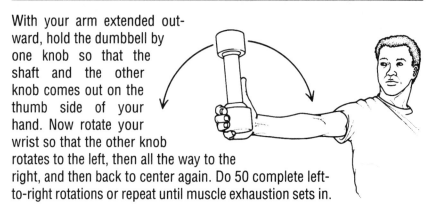

Wrist

Roll-Up

Tie a piece of rope about 3 feet long to the center of a broom or mop handle. Hang a 5-pound dumbbell from the rope. Roll the rope up on the handle as if it were a spool and then roll it back down. Keep your thumbs and index fingers off the handle to keep them out of the exercise so that you do all of the work with the last three fingers of each hand. Repeat until fatigued. Increase the weight as needed.

Ball Squeezing

Hold a soft rubber ball and squeeze it continually until your hand is fatigued. Sporting goods stores also carry a substance called hand putty, which can be squeezed in the same way.

EXTREME GOLF

If you pride yourself in playing quickly and absolutely hate 5-hour rounds, then speed golf (a form of extreme golf) may be for you. Speed golfers sprint from shot to shot with just a handful of clubs, aiming to complete 18 holes in less than an hour.

Playing mainly in Southern California, Florida, and in some areas of the Midwest, manic golfers literally run the course. Running times are added to golf scores for a total. It takes more than endurance to excel. You can be a great runner, but if you lose all of your balls quickly, you're

Strength Workout for Golf

The following chart shows you the benefits of using various exercise machines to improve the strength of specific body parts. You can find these exercise machines at most health clubs. A personal trainer can help you adapt these for your individual needs.

Body Part	Benefit	Exercise
Buttocks and lower back	Driving power, walking endurance	Hip and back machine
Quadriceps	Driving power, walking endurance	Leg Extension
Hamstrings	Hip turn, driving power	Leg Curl
Chest	Club control, impact velocity	Double shoulder lateral press
Triceps and chest	Shoulder turn, club extension	Seated press
Upper back	Shoulder turn, club extension	Pull Over
Forearm flexors	Club control, impact power, acceleration	Wrist Curl
Forearm extensors	Club control, impact power, acceleration	Reverse Wrist Curl

disqualified. The best speed golfers not only run fast but shoot scores in the 70s.

Speed golf has several different sponsors, including PowerBar, and its own association (the Speed Golf Association; call 619-793-2711, ext. 102 for information about membership), with dozens of tournaments scheduled annually around the country.

I think speed golf is a good idea. It reminds me of interval, or circuit, training, where you keep your heart rate in the training range by moving quickly from one exercise activity or machine to the next. It allows you to get some cardiovascular exercise and conditioning from what basically is a noncardiovascular sport.

Go out late one afternoon on a private course and see how well you can do. Make sure, however, that you are in adequate physical condition to play speed golf by first building up some cardiovascular fitness. If you don't do aerobic exercise regularly, the golf course is not a good place to start. In fact, golf courses are hot spots for heart attacks. So warm up and stretch before you take off at top speed and start whacking the ball.

Another form of extreme golf is winter golf. My feeling is that if the course allows you on, play as long into the winter as you wish. Make sure to wear layered clothes and a warm hat to combat the cold. Specially designed winter golf gloves remind me of the gloves pro football players wear in cold weather. You can also take along cart mitts, which are big, furry mittens to be worn in between shots.

Many ski resorts offer winter golf packages in hopes of attracting people year-round. Some even sponsor snowshoe golf tournaments played on flat terrain near the ski slopes. You wear snowshoes instead of golf shoes and hit tennis balls with your golf clubs. Sounds like fun, but it probably only attracts those who can't put down their clubs even in the dead of winter.

2

Eat to Compete

The old adage "You are what you eat" is true when it comes to golf. Fill your diet with high-fat foods and you are likely to increase your weight—and your golf scores. On the other hand, eating a healthy diet chockful of complex carbohydrates provides your body with the energy it needs to sustain even long, five-hour rounds.

What's the best thing for golfers to eat? Should you have coffee and donuts before an early morning tee time? How about a hot dog and beer at the turn? Most dietary advice buzzed around the clubhouse is exaggerated, inaccurate, or downright harmful. This chapter dispels some of those myths and offers solid advice on how to build a better body for golf:

- What to eat in the off-season
- What to eat before, during, and after a round
- What to drink before, during, and after a round

OFF-SEASON NUTRITION

Weight control is most important to better golf. Carrying around excess weight can cause fatigue if you are walking the course. This is particularly noticeable on a hilly course or on hot, humid days. Being overweight also decreases your ability to adequately rotate the body properly for a powerful swing. A large abdomen and chest interfere with the position of the arms on the backswing and follow-through.

The off-season is a good time to control weight. To do that, you need to consume fewer calories and eat a low-fat diet. Fat (with 9 calories per gram) has more than twice as many calories as carbohydrates and proteins (4 calories per gram). Weight loss depends on a simple equation: calories in should be less than calories out. By reducing the calorie intake of your diet and increasing your calorie expenditure with exercise, you will lose weight.

A weight loss of 1 to 2 pounds of fat per week through combined diet and exercise is feasible. If you drop any more weight than that, you are probably losing muscle and fluid, not body fat.

To perform your best on the golf course, you should eat a balanced diet of low-fat, moderate-protein, high-carbohydrate foods and beverages; snack on high-carbohydrate, low-fat foods; and drink plenty of fluids. Good nutrition can help you reach your athletic potential.

Within a balanced diet, choose these lower-fat items whenever possible:

- A slice of whole wheat bread, an English muffin, a bagel, or a non-granola cereal without nuts or seeds, such as Cheerios, Wheaties, or corn flakes.

- Fresh, whole fruits, which are better for weight loss because they contain more fiber than juices; 100 percent fruit juice rather than juice drinks.

- Low-fat dairy products such as skim or 1 percent milk.

- Brightly colored vegetables and fresh or frozen vegetables without added fat, because they have more vitamins and are more nutritious.

- Fish, seafood, and poultry more often than beef and other red meats. Eat lean cuts of well-trimmed meat with little marbling. Have poultry without the skin and nonbreaded and nonfried whenever possible.

- Reduced-fat margarine, mayonnaise, and salad dressing. Use canola or olive oil and salad dressing without cream or cheese. Take in fat primarily in the form of fish, canola oil, or olive oil.

A diet high in complex carbohydrates, moderate in proteins, and low in fats can also help keep your energy level up during a weight-loss program. Carbohydrates also have a fair amount of fiber, so they fill you up with fewer calories. A lot of fatty foods contain fat and fat-soluble vitamins, but nothing else. Many foods high in carbohydrates have small amounts of protein and a number of vitamins and minerals. Sources of carbohydrates include breads, cereals, grains, and other starches such as potatoes, corn, milk, beans, peas, lentils, fruits and fruit juices, and vegetables.

KNOW WHAT TO EAT BEFORE, DURING, AND AFTER A ROUND

Before Hitting a Ball

In general, you should eat at least 2 hours before playing. Before a big match, because of added anxiety, allow more time than normal, about 3 to 4 hours. Being nervous slows down digestion, and you may become more aware of stomach upset. This may be tolerable during a practice session or your regular game, but it could affect your performance in a tournament.

Before going out on the course, eat a high-carbohydrate meal. I prefer a bowl of high-fiber cereal, fruit, and low-fat milk. This is especially important if you have an early tee time. Golfers have a tendency to skip breakfast to make an early start. Big mistake. Without any food intake since the night before, all ready sources of energy have already been depleted. Basically, you need to leave enough time so that food empties from your stomach, yet eat close enough to your tee time to prevent hunger and exhaustion later on.

Avoid high-fat foods before playing. Skip the egg-and-sausage sandwich on a croissant, the cheese danish, or donuts. Opt for a bagel with low-fat cream cheese or jelly instead. Foods high in fat slow the emptying time of the stomach by several hours. The body responds to exercising muscles by sending them an increased supply of blood that contains nutrients. However, the intestinal tract gets first priority after you have eaten. So a full stomach gets the increased blood supply to aid digestion, not the muscles.

Good energy sources are particularly important for those who are walking the course. Golfers who ride an electric cart will not notice the energy loss as much since they will burn fewer calories.

During the Round

Because of the length of time on the course and the energy expended, many golfers become hungry and find it necessary to eat something. Good, virtually noiseless on-the-course foods are bagels (again), bananas (which are high in potassium), oranges (which help quench thirst), and jelly sandwiches (which are low in fat). Don't add peanut butter to the jelly sandwich. Not only does it contain fat and make you thirsty, it's hard to yell "Fore" with peanut butter stuck to the roof of your mouth. And don't make any sandwich with mayonnaise, which spoils quickly in the heat.

Avoid eating heavy foods the last few holes, even if you are very hungry. A high-energy bar is a good choice, and a much better choice than a candy bar. High-energy bars are derivatives of granola bars with much of the fat removed and more carbohydrates added in. Nutritionally, they are far superior to candy bars.

Candy bars taste good, but they have several drawbacks. Their high-fat content contributes to delayed emptying of the stomach. This not only reduces the amount of energy available to working muscles, but delays needed energy from reaching the muscles. Candy bars also rely on sugar for energy rather than complex carbohydrates. A sudden increase in circulating blood sugar causes the body to respond by producing increased insulin. This overproduction of insulin results in a lowering of blood sugar, the exact opposite of what the golfer intended, and quickly leads to fatigue.

The 19th Hole

After playing, replace the calories burned during the round with a good, balanced meal. The food should include enough protein to allow tissues to repair themselves after exercising. The average American eats seven times as much protein as is necessary, so most golfers do not need to eat anything extra or insist on a steak. The amount of calories replaced depends on the amount of energy expended, which is generally based on whether the golfer walked or rode. A golfer who walks 18 holes may burn between 1,000 calories (pulling a cart) to 2,000 calories (carrying a bag).

There is no special diet for golfers. Most of the replacement calories after playing should come from complex carbohydrates, such as potatoes, bread, green vegetables, and fruit. Again, try to avoid fats and sweets.

KNOW WHAT TO DRINK BEFORE, DURING, AND AFTER A ROUND

A golfer's concerns about fluid intake and hydration depend on heat and humidity. An increase in either temperature or humidity can cause body heat problems. Humidity is more important than temperature. However, a day with high temperature and low humidity may be deceiving. Sweat evaporates so rapidly that the golfer may not be aware of fluid loss. With high humidity, sweat evaporates more slowly, so at least the golfer is more aware of sweating.

In high temperature and high humidity, golfers need to begin drinking approximately 1 hour before teeing off—about 8 ounces of liquid every 20 minutes. During your warm-up, drink cold water. Cold water empties from the stomach faster than warm water. If you have stomach cramps, it's probably from taking too much water at once. If you experience cramps, try warm water or fluids with salt or sugar in them.

Drink water at every water stop available on the course, if not on every tee, if possible. You can carry a water bottle with you, or attach a special cooler that holds liquids to your bag. Don't wait until thirst sets in. You will never catch up. Continue to take in liquids after coming off the course. Avoid caffeinated beverages and alcoholic drinks, including beer, because they act as diuretics. Plain old water works best.

As the body depletes its supply of fluid, muscles lose their flexibility and strength. The end result of fluid deprivation can be heat exhaustion and heat stroke. If you are going to play daily in a hot, humid climate, such as on a golf vacation, weigh yourself daily. If your weight stays constant, you are replacing lost liquids adequately.

It takes about 7 to 10 days to acclimate to heat. After that, the body learns to conserve fluids. Unfortunately, most golf vacations last just about that long, so be aware of losing weight rapidly. A golfer who loses more than 3 pounds of body weight over a few days may be in the process of becoming dehydrated, and runs the risk of having difficulty with muscle cramps and heat illness (see chapter 4). Drinking more than the normal amount of water can get the weight back up.

ELECTROLYTE REPLACEMENT

A loss of electrolytes (salt and potassium) leads to muscle cramping and fatigue. You need some salt to compensate for sweat losses, but there is no place for salt pills in golf, or any sport for that matter. A large amount of salt in the intestines causes the body to extract large amounts of water from the body tissues to dilute it, causing further dehydration in the muscles.

In hot weather, simply increase the salt intake in your food. Salty foods like pickles and relish are good. Also, eat more high potassium foods, such as bananas, tomatoes, melons, and skim milk. These high-potassium foods are also good because they are great sources of carbo-hydrates and proteins, contain no fat, and provide lots of vitamins and minerals.

Sports drinks contain all of the electrolytes, plus liquid and glucose, necessary for energy replacement. However, they are expensive if taken frequently, and probably are no more effective than water in a low-intensity sport like golf. It's probably best to drink water on the course and, if you like the taste of sports drinks, have them after coming off the course to immediately replace any lost electrolytes.

If you feel muscle cramps coming on, say at the end of 36 holes on a desert course, have a sports drink plus water. Rehydrating early enough can stop muscle cramps and allow you to complete the round.

Part Two

Common Risks and Basic Safeguards

Golf Injuries and Rehabilitation

Medical Risks

Health Gadgets

Golf Injuries
and Rehabilitation

Although most people would agree that golf is not a rigorous sport, it cannot be considered an innocuous one. I have seen a wide range of muscular and skeletal ailments among amateur and professional golfers. Considering the large, repetitive forces generated by a club head traveling about 100 miles per hour in less than one-fifth of a second, it's no wonder golfers become injured.

This chapter shows when injuries occur during the swing, the predisposing factors for injuries, and outlines a program to help you recover from golf injuries. As you will see in the following chapters, most golf injuries are caused by overplaying or overuse, followed by a poor swing, hitting an object other than the ball, or an inadequate warm-up.

THE SWING

The primary objective of a golfer executing a full swing is to produce maximum distance, accuracy, and control when hitting the ball. To achieve maximum club head speed, the whole body has to be put into action. Each body part acts as a link in the chain of events. This allows you to generate and transfer energy from the legs and trunk to the back, shoulders, elbows, and wrists as you go through the swing.

The more efficient the golfer's biomechanics are in each stage of the swing, the less risk of injury. On the other hand, poor biomechanics or muscular weakness or inflexibility increases the risk of injury. So it is important to look at the overall biomechanics of the swing and also at each link in the chain.

Bob, a 49-year-old accountant and avid golfer, came to see me with a recurrent pain in his right wrist. After examining him, I found that his wrist was sore and swollen, and prescribed rest and some anti-inflammatory drugs. Two weeks later, he was back in my office with the same complaint. I asked him to go through the swing motion for me, and could see that his lower back was very stiff. The back stiffness was forcing him to overswing to get the club into the proper position at the top of the backswing. We discussed a simple back stretching program, which Bob did religiously. For the rest of the golf season, he had no more wrist pain, and told me, "I've added 10 yards to my drives now that I'm turning more freely."

THREE SWING PHASES

To examine when a golfer becomes injured, let's look at the three phases of the golf swing—the take-away, the downswing, and the follow-through.

The take-away, or setting up to the top of the backswing, causes 25 percent of injuries and places stress on the golfer's back, shoulders, and arms. As a right-handed golfer rotates the knees, hips, lower back, and spine, the head remains relatively stationary, and the weight shifts to the right side. The left arm comes across the trunk and the left thumb cocks and rotates as the right wrist flexes.

The downswing, pre-impact and impact, leads to 50 percent of injuries because this phase of the swing generates the greatest forces. The range of motion is the same as the take-away, but the body moves about three times as fast. This can lead to injuries in buttocks, quadriceps, hamstrings, and lower back muscles, as well as the wrists and knees. The weight shifts to the left from the counterclockwise torque of the buttocks, quadriceps, hamstrings, and lower back muscles. The wrists remain cocked, with the right wrist at its maximum flex. The left thumb is cocked and pointed away from the palm. The nerves and muscles in the forearm and elbow are under tension.

The follow-through causes 25 percent of injuries, with most of the injuries in this phase due to the extension of the golfer's back into the modern reverse-C position at the finish. The left forearm and right forearm turn toward the ball as the lower back and spine rotate and extend to their limits. The right knee flexes as the left knee turns outward and the hips rotate completely.

PROS VERSUS AMATEURS

Few studies have been conducted about the incidence of golf injuries, but surveys of amateur and professional golfers have found that the areas most commonly injured are the lower back, elbow, hand, wrist, shoulder, and knee. Professional golfers are more likely to have the highest number of injuries in the wrist, followed by the back, hand, shoulder, and knee. In contrast, amateurs suffer mostly from lower back injuries, followed by the elbow, wrist, shoulder, and knee.

PREDISPOSING FACTORS

A combination of factors predispose the amateur golfer to injury, including age, biomechanics, and training mistakes.

With advanced age, there is an obvious increased susceptibility to degenerative diseases. In the golfer, these most commonly are joint diseases of the neck, lower back, hip, and knee, as well as tendon tears in the rotator cuff within the shoulder or in the elbow. For some golfers, golf may be an incidental or aggravating factor. For others, it may be a significant factor that leads to the development of severe symptoms.

Any variation from the so-called ideal swing can bring about increased stress to muscles, tendons, and bones. These variations are quite common and more pronounced among amateur golfers. As a result, an assessment of your swing by a professional may be the most important step in preventing golf injuries. The use of video analysis is particularly useful in checking your biomechanics.

The cumulative effect of repetitive, tiny traumas throughout the body while playing and practicing can eventually lead to overuse injuries, such as rotator cuff tears, golfer's elbow, wrist and hand tendinitis, and even stress fractures of the ribs. It is said that perfect practice leads to perfection. But imperfect practice often leads to injury.

Golfers are also susceptible to a peculiar mix of illnesses and injuries as a direct result of their environment and equipment. Being hit by errant golf balls or broken shafts can lead to cuts and bruises, broken bones, or even a concussion from a blow to the head. For example, mishit shots—hitting the ground hard instead of the ball—can lead to hand fractures, wrist damage, and severe elbow injuries. Heat, sun, lightning, pollens, agricultural chemicals, insects, birds, reptiles, and plants in the environment can contribute to a variety of illnesses, some of them life-threatening, such as heat stroke, others annoying, like insect bites (see chapter 4).

REHABILITATION OF GOLF INJURIES

The rehabilitation of golf injuries should ensure the full restoration of function of both the injured area as well as each link in the swing chain. When necessary, I send injured golfers for physical therapy for massage, joint mobilization, electrical stimulation, and exercises to restore full range of motion, flexibility, and strength. However, you can rehabilitate most golf injuries on your own.

A gradual return to activity and avoiding any previous training errors are important to prevent any reinjuries. Avoiding excessive practice, along with improved biomechanics, should reduce your incidence of golf injuries.

The following monthlong rehabilitation program should get you back on the course after a golf injury. A good warm-up is an essential part of any sports activity, including golfing. So warm up for 10 minutes before going through your rehabilitation routine.

Week	Monday	Wednesday	Friday
1	10 minutes putt 5 minutes chip 5 minutes rest 5 minutes chip	Same as Monday	Same as Monday
2	5 minutes putt 10 minutes chip 5 minutes rest 5 minutes short irons	5 minutes putt 10 minutes chip 5 minutes rest 10 minutes short irons	5 minutes putt 10 minutes chip 5 minutes rest 10 minutes short irons 5 minutes rest 10 minutes short irons
3	5 minutes chip 15 minutes short irons 5 minutes rest 10 minutes long irons 5 minutes rest 10 minutes long irons	5 minutes chip 15 minutes short irons 5 minutes rest 15 minutes long irons 5 minutes rest 10 minutes woods	5 minutes chip 15 minutes short irons 5 minutes rest 15 minutes long irons 5 minutes rest 15 minutes woods
4	Play 9 holes	Play 9 holes	Play more holes if you can

USE THE RIGHT PAINKILLERS

Painkilling medications can allow golfers to start aggressive, early rehabilitation of injuries.

Aspirin, such as Bayer, is the oldest and probably most widely prescribed drug. It not only kills pain but also reduces inflammation. The major side effect of aspirin is stomach upset and even bleeding from the lining of the stomach. If you have problems with regular aspirin, use buffered or enteric-coated aspirin instead.

Acetaminophen pills, such as Tylenol, have the same painkilling effects as aspirin in most people but do not have as much of an anti-inflammatory effect. Some people find them less irritating to the stomach.

Ibuprofen, such as Advil, is the active ingredient in nonsteroidal anti-inflammatory agents. The various over-the-counter preparations are half-strength versions of prescription medications. They all have a very strong anti-inflammatory effect and also have pain-relieving properties.

Anti-inflammatories must be taken carefully. They can have severe gastrointestinal (GI) side effects; they may irritate the stomach and cause bleeding as well as ulcers. They can interfere with the production of the coating that protects the stomach and intestine from stomach acid. Anyone with a history of GI problems should not take anti-inflammatory agents, including those sold in drugstores, except under a doctor's direction. The doctor may prescribe accompanying medication to ameliorate the side effects.

I usually let golfers in pain choose whichever painkiller they like best. Most of them know from previous experience which drug works well for them. The only caveat is not to take aspirin along with anti-inflammatory agents. Since these two are chemically similar, adding one to the other could lead to a toxic reaction. So, for example, if you are taking ibuprofen for sore muscles and you get a headache, take acetaminophen instead of aspirin.

USE FIRST AID FOR COMMON MUSCLE INJURIES

How to Treat Muscle Pulls

No matter how diligently you warm up and stretch, or warm down and stretch, you may still pull a muscle from overuse, fatigue, or injury. A muscle pull occurs when a sudden, severe force is applied to the muscle and the fibers are stretched beyond their capacity. If most of the fibers are overstretched and a few are torn, you have a muscle pull. If many of the fibers tear, it becomes a muscle tear, which is rare in golf.

The universal treatment for a muscle pull or tear is to apply ice. This relaxes the muscle and helps relieve any spasm. Apply ice to the injured body part and rest it until the pain and swelling subside. You should apply the ice for about 20 minutes at a time for several days to reduce inflammation. Then you can start rehabilitating the body part with a gentle exercise and stretching program.

You must stretch the muscle while it heals. A pulled muscle usually goes into spasm, which is a protective mechanism that causes the stretched muscle fibers to contract. If the fibers are not gradually re-lengthened, the muscle will pull again once you return to play because it will have healed in a shortened state. If you stretch the healing muscle gradually, not violently, you will decrease your chance of reinjuring it.

In general, you can return to action when you are able to stretch the injured body part without pain as far as you can stretch the healthy one on the other side of the body.

How to Treat Muscle Spasms

If you show up on Monday at your doctor's office because you "threw your back out" playing golf over the weekend, you may have a delayed muscle spasm rather than torn muscle fibers. Most muscle injuries result in some degree of spasm or tightness. In fact, many mild muscle "pulls" actually end up to be low-grade spasms. If you are not sure when the muscle began to hurt, you probably have not torn the muscle.

Some doctors like to give painkillers or anti-inflammatory agents as soon as possible after a muscle spasm starts and then suggest that the golfer rest. Rather than keep my patients out of action with total rest, I prefer to get them involved in a gradual exercise program that uses a combination of icing and stretching.

First, apply a large cold pack to the muscle to numb it. A good way to do this is to make an ice cone by freezing water in a styrofoam cup and peel down the rim, and then rub the muscle with the ice until it is numb.

Next, start moving the sore muscle until you begin to feel tightness or pain. When the pain disappears, hold the injured body part in that position for a 20-second static stretch. A few moments later, contract the muscle slowly but fully, and hold for about 5 seconds. This isometric contraction will help relax the muscle more.

Now, move the body part again until you feel tightness or pain. Hold the body part for 10 seconds and then contract the muscle for 5 seconds. Repeat the stretch and contraction again, and then stretch the muscle one last time.

Let the body part rest naturally for 20 seconds and repeat the entire program. You may need to re-numb the muscle between sessions.

This method of icing and stretching can also be used initially in muscle pulls and tears. Within two or three days, the dull ache of the muscle spasm will be partially relieved. Then you can gradually resume playing again.

How to Treat Sore Muscles

Delayed muscle soreness and pain typically occur a day or two after strenuous exercise. A golfer may feel it after several days of a 36-hole-per-day golf excursion. The soreness usually subsides by itself within a few days. Mild exercise and liniment may help relive the soreness.

There are two basic types of liniment you can buy in a drugstore. The first includes products such as Ben-Gay and Sports Creme, which typically contain menthol and an aspirin-like chemical, methyl salicylate. When you rub it in, your skin becomes slightly irritated, which causes an increase in blood flow to the area. This also produces heat, which relaxes stiff muscles. These rubs may also allow some salicylate to enter the bloodstream. Since salicylate is the active ingredient in aspirin, they may also have some pain-relieving effect.

The second type of rub, including Hot-Stuff and Atomic Balm, depends on a substance called capsicum, which is the active ingredient in jalapeño peppers. An extract of this chemical is now being used as an ointment for arthritis pain, which is an indication that these rubs really do work. These hotter rubs have a much stronger irritating effect on the skin to stimulate blood flow. They give off so much heat that you can actually burn yourself, especially if you have fair skin. Go slowly when you use them until you can see how your skin reacts.

In addition to its use as an exercise rub, liniment is touted by some manufacturers as a warm-up aid. Liniment can help relax tight muscles and increase circulation. It may shorten your warm-up time, particularly in cold weather, and may help increase blood flow after warm-down to reduce the lactic acid residue.

But don't think that because you have applied liniment you are warmed up. A proper warm-up raises overall body temperature, not just the temperature in one muscle group. Think of liniment as a passive warm-up for one body part. Combine it with 10 minutes of light exercise, followed by stretching, to warm up the whole body.

Aspirin may be helpful in relieving muscle soreness. Several studies have found that taking aspirin after exercise reduces muscle soreness and improves range of motion a day or two later.

For additional first-aid tips, look for this symbol throughout the book:

4

Medical Risks

Besides injuries, golfers are subject to other medical problems related to the game. The previous chapter gave you specific information about who gets injured. This chapter looks at other risks to your health and how to deal with them, including:

- Prevent Body Heat Problems

- Avoid Sun Exposure

- On-the-Course Health Hazards

- Relieving Respiratory Problems

PREVENT BODY HEAT PROBLEMS

The body has three cooling mechanisms: radiation, convection, and evaporation.

Radiation depends on the ability of the body to emit heat. As your body temperature rises, the small blood vessels (capillaries) in the skin dilate. This is why your skin turns red. Large quantities of blood rise to the skin surface where heat can be radiated to the outside to cool off the body. This increase in blood flow to the skin allows the heat to dissipate. However, exercising muscles demand large quantities of blood to supply oxygen and fuel. This reduces the amount of blood available to the skin, so radiation becomes less effective.

Convection depends upon the difference between your body temperature and the air temperature to transfer heat from the body. As the air temperature rises toward normal body temperature, the temperature difference decreases, and less heat is drawn off the body. So convection becomes less effective as the weather gets hotter.

Evaporation is the best source of heat loss. The evaporation of sweat is a cooling process. The higher the temperature, the more the body responds by increasing its sweating. But high humidity interferes with this process: more moisture in the air means that less sweat evaporates. With no evaporation, there is no cooling. So playing golf on a humid day may be more dangerous than on a hot one. Also, if you keep perspiring without replacing body fluids, you become dehydrated. Excessive sweating leads to loss of body salts and potassium, which are collectively known as electrolytes.

What you wear can improve the effectiveness of cooling mechanisms. The more skin exposed to the air, the more heat you allow to leave your body through the skin. Natural fibers transmit heat and allow evaporation better than artificial fibers. Light clothes reflect external heat better than dark clothes. Covering the body with clothing that does not provide good heat conduction can be dangerous and lead to heat exhaustion or heat stroke.

Golfers have a choice to make on a hot, humid day. Exposing as much of the body as possible allows you to handle the heat better. Yet covering up as much as possible helps avoid exposure to the sun, as well as exposure to tick and insect bites. I prefer to wear a wide-brimmed hat, lightweight, light-colored cotton shorts, and short-sleeved shirts during the dog days of summer, with plenty of sunscreen and insect spray, and just avoid going into the woods after balls to avoid the ticks.

Heat Exhaustion

Heat exhaustion is due to dehydration and the loss of electrolytes. It causes you to feel light-headed and dizzy, and you may even faint. Your cooling mechanisms are working overtime so that you are sweaty, and your skin is cool and clammy. You may also have severe muscle cramps due to the loss of salt and potassium. If you experience these symptoms, stop playing or practicing, rest in a cool place, and replace your fluids with water or an electrolyte drink, such as Gatorade. In severe cases, you may need to have fluids and electrolytes replaced intravenously at a hospital emergency room.

[EMERGENCY] *Heatstroke*

Heatstroke is a true medical emergency. In this case, all of the heat mechanisms have failed, and the body temperature has risen to the point where the brain's regulating mechanism has been knocked out. Body temperatures may go as high as 107 to 109°F. The symptoms of heatstroke are red, hot skin; lack of sweating; and, usually, loss of consciousness. Get someone with heatstroke to the emergency room immediately, where an ice bath, ice packs, or a cooling blanket can be used to help lower the body temperature. Someone with heatstroke could die very quickly without treatment.

Preventing Heat Problems

You can prevent heat problems by watching the weather and your fluid intake. In hot weather, you may lose up to one-half gallon of sweat per hour while on the course.

Check the temperature and humidity before you go out to play. If the temperature and humidity are both high, wait until they have both gone down, or simply play fewer holes. Try to play early in the morning or the evening when temperatures are generally lower. Walk under trees or get into the shade whenever possible. While I don't generally recommend using an electric cart, you might consider taking one with a roof in very hot weather to provide some shade and help protect you from dehydration.

To keep fluid intake up, take frequent water breaks, at least every 15 minutes, if not every hole. Carry a bottle filled with plain water or an electrolyte drink, such as Gatorade, in your bag or cart. Do not take salt tablets. They cause the body to extract large amounts of water to dilute the excess salt, which only causes more dehydration in the muscles.

AVOID SUN EXPOSURE

The sun's radiation has strengthened in recent years as the earth's protective atmospheric ozone layer has thinned. Heedless of warnings about exposure to the sun and the cancer risk it poses, millions of golfers play the game without protective clothing or sunscreens. But skin cancer is making an unexpected reappearance and should give any golfer pause before heading for the course. The sun also affects the eyes, and sunglasses with UV protection are a must on bright, sunny days.

Skin Cancer

About one in six Americans will have skin cancer, and about 1 million new cases are diagnosed each year. The most common types of skin cancer are directly related to sun exposure, which put golfers at risk because they spend so much time in the sun.

There are three types of skin cancer: squamous cell cancer, basal cell cancer, and malignant melanoma. Skin cancer is usually a culmination of many years of exposure to the sun. It is usually more common in fair-skinned people, who have a low pigment content in their skin. Sun damage is permanent, and just one blistering sunburn before the age of 20 doubles the risk of skin cancer for the rest of your life.

Squamous cell cancer and basal cell cancer usually present as a persistent pimple or ulcer that will not heal. The skin may crust over, but it will open again. Squamous cell cancer is more common on the ear and lower lip, but may spread throughout the body. Basal cell cancer is most common on exposed areas of the skin and is not likely to spread, but it can be very destructive to the skin. If caught early, virtually all squamous cell and basal cell cancers are curable with surgical removal.

Malignant melanoma is an aggressive skin cancer that may occur anywhere, but usually appears on an exposed surface of the body. It can spread to other body parts, where it usually is lethal. Signs of melanoma include an unusual-looking black mole that suddenly appears, or a persistent mole that suddenly enlarges.

Unless diagnosed early and widely removed, melanoma can be rapidly fatal. Traces of melanoma may lie dormant in someone who had had a skin tumor removed, and then crop up decades later. About four in five people who have a melanoma removed from their skin survive another 10 years without a recurrence.

Melanoma is increasing in sunny regions that have large white populations, such as the U.S. Southwest. Between 1980 and the mid-1990s, the incidence of melanoma in the United States has doubled. More than 40,000 people are diagnosed with melanoma each year. Although regular skin examinations have saved many lives, more than 7,300 Americans die from melanoma each year.

Who Is at Risk?

If you have more than 20 moles or a family history of skin cancer, you may want to see a dermatologist for regular checkups. If you live in a hot, sunny climate, more ultraviolet rays may reach your skin, making you more susceptible to skin cancer. Melanoma may occur more frequently in those who have occasional, intense sun exposure.

There are signs you can watch for. These include new or changing spots, especially those that are asymmetrical, have irregular borders or bumpy surfaces, vary in color, or are larger than a pencil eraser. I recommend that every golfer do a careful self-examination of the entire body before and after the golf season to detect any changes in existing moles.

Preventing Skin Cancer

Protective clothing and liberal use of sunscreens are very important, particularly if you play golf several times a week. Anyone who plays in a climate with a strong tropical sun should take proper precautions.

A broad-brimmed hat protects the back of the neck and ears, which are highly susceptible areas. Darker clothes and hats block more dangerous ultraviolet rays than light-colored ones. A denim shirt has a sun protection factor (SPF) of 1,700, but a light-colored, cotton golf shirt has an SPF of just 8.

Sunscreen takes 20 to 30 minutes to begin working, so apply sunscreen at least 30 minutes before heading outside. Wear a sunscreen with an SPF of at least 15, and if you are out in the sun for more than 4 hours, reapply the sunscreen. The lips are especially vulnerable to sunburn, so use special lip sunscreens as well.

Selecting a Sunscreen

Each person's need for sunscreen is different, depending on skin type and the duration of time spent in the sun. Selecting the proper product doesn't have to be confusing despite all the different SPF numbers on the labels and a dizzying array of ingredients. Each of the products is a little bit different, so it might take a bit of experimentation to find the product that is best for you.

The SPF, incidentally, tells you how long the product is expected to protect your skin from burning. For example, a 15 SPF sunscreen should protect your skin from developing redness 15 times longer than no sunscreen at all. However, the reality is that thorough, frequent application of sunscreen is as important as the SPF rating.

If you follow the instructions on the bottle, using sunscreen correctly is easy. Here are some suggestions:

- Apply sunscreen thoroughly and evenly. The average adult needs about 2 tablespoons spread evenly over the entire body.

- Don't agonize over the SPF number. Most people should use an SPF of 15 if their skin is normal, or an SPF of 30 if they are taking photosensitizing medications (such as certain blood pressure pills) or suffering from a disease (such as lupus) that would make their skin unusually susceptible to burns. SPF numbers lower than 15 probably won't offer enough protection, while those higher than 30 may not offer any additional benefits.

- Buy a waterproof sunscreen. It won't be washed off quickly by your own sweat, and so is useful even if you're not going swimming.

- Check the label to make sure your sunscreen protects against both ultraviolet A (UVA) and ultraviolet B (UVB) light, since sunlight contains both types of ultraviolet rays.

- Be alert for sunscreen allergies, which may show up as rashes. If you have a skin reaction, switch to a brand with different ingredients. Generally, sunblocks with titanium dioxide are less likely to cause allergic skin reactions. Most sunblocks work by absorbing light, but the "physical" sunblocks, such as titanium dioxide, work by reflecting and scattering the sun's rays. Also, the fragrance or

preservatives in a sunscreen can cause irritation, so simply changing brands (regardless of active ingredients) can sometimes be effective.

- If you are extremely sensitive to sunlight, use zinc oxide or an equivalent "sunblock" that keeps out all light. You no longer have to live
  with that white, pasty look with the introduction of new zinc sunblocks that come in fluorescent colors.

Eye Problems

Golfers need to wear sunglasses for the same reason they apply sunscreen: harmful ultraviolet light can also affect the eyes. Ultraviolet light
levels are typically higher from late spring through the summer—the
peak golf season.

Sunlight that reflects off the sand and the grass can burn cells on the
eye's surface. A few years of sun exposure can cause unsightly, fleshy
growths called pterygiums on the whites of the eyes. Usually harmless,
they sometimes spread over the iris and interfere with vision.

A lifetime of playing golf without eye protection increases your risk
for some serious ailments. Over the years, ultraviolet rays damage the
eye's lens. Proteins in the lens may form milky clouds known as
cataracts. Lens surgery can often restore vision loss from cataracts.

Cataracts are known to occur more frequently in tropical or sunny
climates. Prolonged exposure to sunlight is definitely a risk factor
in the formation of cataracts. The definitive study was conducted
on Chesapeake Bay fishermen over a 20-year period. The fishermen
who wore sunglasses had a much lower incidence of cataracts than
those who did not. The Johns Hopkins researchers who conducted the
study advise wearing a hat with a brim and close-fitting sunglasses
with ultraviolet-absorbing lenses. In a follow-up study, they found that
a lifetime of moderate sun exposure may be as dangerous as a few
years of intense exposure.

Ultraviolet light may also injure the macula, an area of the eye that
enables you to see fine details. If lesions form—a condition called macu-
lar degeneration—this type of vision is irretrievably lost.

Protecting the Eyes

Good sunglasses help keep your eyes healthy. The lenses should block at least 99 percent of ultraviolet rays. The color or tint of the lenses is unimportant as long as they block ultraviolet rays. A polarized lens will also reduce glare off the sand or the grass. Wraparound or large-frame glasses block more light, and wraparounds prevent light from seeping in from the sides, as David Duval knows.

A handful of manufacturers—including Bollé, Oakley, and Cobra Golf—now make sunglasses specifically for golf. From ultracool wraparounds to classic aviators, these sunglasses are generally lightweight, shatter-resistant, adjustable, and offer distortion-free lenses that keep out wind and glare. Most of them allow you to incorporate your prescription into the lenses or fit prescription lenses behind the tinted ones. Some of them have interchangeable lenses with different tints. They range in cost from about $30 to $200, and are available in pro shops, sports specialty stores, and department stores, or through mail-order catalogs.

Incidentally, while eye injuries are not common in golf, they are the most severe of any sport. The speed, size, and hardness of the golf ball allows it to penetrate the bone surrounding the eye, known as the orbit. Any direct hit will almost always cause the loss of the eye. Sunglasses also provide a little bit of protection from such an injury.

Eye-care companies are also marketing new contact lenses that block harmful ultraviolet light. These extended-wear contacts, coated with ultraviolet-absorbing chemicals, block up to 90 percent of ultraviolet rays and cost about the same as normal contacts. Like wraparound sunglasses, they do not let light in from the sides.

ON-THE-COURSE HEALTH HAZARDS

When you get to the course, you don't want to be distracted by chemicals on the ground, ticks in the woods, and insects in the air. The game is distracting enough as it is. Here's how to prevent medical problems caused by these on-the-course health hazards.

Reducing Chemical Exposure

To most golfers, chemical use by the local golf course is just one method to keep the grass green and the course in good playing condition. To others, it appears to be a threat to the environment or, even worse, to their own health. In general, golf courses are environmentally friendly, but you should take a few simple precautions to reduce contact with chemicals.

Overall, pesticides provide almost no risk for casual exposure to levels that would be of any concern to golfers. Most pesticides are applied wet, and if they dry before coming into contact with people, they will not easily come off the vegetation. Once the pesticide dries on the leaf of turf grass, you can't just casually brush it off. To get any pesticide residue at all you have to take a rough cloth and vigorously rub the grass leaf. Obviously, no one out playing golf is going to do that in the course of a round.

One good way to reduce exposure to pesticides is to not pressure the golf course to allow golfers to play through areas recently treated with pesticides. There are two main professionals at every golf course, the golf course superintendent and the head golf pro. Their staffs work together to schedule pesticide applications so that there is minimal interference with golfers. The best solution is for you to be more understanding when course maintenance causes a minor interference with a round of golf.

Likewise, the golfer who complains about the stray dandelion or patch of poor turf may pressure the course superintendent to overuse chemicals. Most golfers adapt to courses that are less than perfect. On British-style courses, a few weeds and some brown spots are considered part of the game.

Another way to reduce inadvertent chemical exposure is to ask your golf pro and course superintendent to use practices that reduce exposure. Ask them to post signs at the first tee explaining what pesticides have been applied that day and when. Many courses already do this. Courses also can use equipment, such as spray shrouds, that prevent pesticide drift caused by the wind. They are more likely to do that if they know that pesticide exposure is a concern.

Many golf courses have adopted a combination of organic and chemical applications. Instead of chemicals, they use natural organic material to treat pests and fertilize the soil. It may take a while to catch on, but more courses are changing to reflect people's attitudes toward being environmentally safe.

For those who are concerned about exposure to pesticides and chemical fertilizers and want to restrict their exposure, here are some additional tips:

- Don't move anything from the turf to your mouth. Do not chew on blades of grass or golf tees. Also take care to protect any food you are eating from touching the ground. Cigars are popular now, especially on golf courses, but golfers should avoid placing them on the ground while they take their swings. Not only is there a chance that the cigar will come into direct contact with the chemicals, but some courses are irrigated with wastewater from sewage treatment plants, so there's a chance of bacterial contamination as well.

  Several products have recently appeared that prevent cigars from hitting the turf. One is a small plastic holder that attaches to a golf tee and can be placed in the ground; another is an aluminum cigar holder that attaches to the handle of a golf bag. These products may be found in cigar and golf stores and catalogs.

- Talk to the course superintendent to find out what chemicals were applied and when. Most golf courses apply chemicals in the early mornings through the week; they are rarely applied on weekends.

- Wash your hands and forearms at the end of a round.

- Wear long pants whenever the weather allows.

- Avoid playing on days when pesticides or fertilizers have been applied to the turf.

- Never play golf in your bare feet.

Golf Ball Liver

Most pesticides are severely toxic to the liver. Recently, a new golf-related hazard was identified as "golf ball liver." In Ireland, a 65-year-old retired engineer who played golf every day experienced lethargy and abdominal discomfort, had dark urine and jaundice, and was finally diagnosed with acute hepatitis. The cause was a mystery until his doctor discovered that he often licked his golf balls to clean them. His habit exposed him to the weed killer used on the greens, which was 2,4-D, better known as Agent Orange. He did this despite signs warning that the greens were regularly treated with potentially toxic weed killers.

Following his doctor's orders, the patient ceased using his tongue to clean his golf balls, and his symptoms faded. But the man may have remained privately skeptical regarding his diagnosis. When the golf course was resprayed with the weed killer, he resumed licking his golf ball to rechallenge himself for a month, and his hepatitis symptoms returned. The man now cleans his balls with a damp cloth.

Tick Bites

As summer heats up and you head to the links more often, you need to take precautions to avoid tick-borne illnesses such as Lyme disease and Rocky Mountain spotted fever. These diseases are easily treatable when diagnosed early. However, they are often misdiagnosed or missed until severe symptoms appear because golfers don't think much about them.

Lyme Disease

Lyme disease is usually caused by a bite from an infected deer tick. These ticks are most prevalent in the northeastern part of the United States. The disease is more prevalent during moist, humid seasons, and the incidence drops during dry seasons. A bite by a Lyme-infected tick will cause a rash that characteristically looks like a bull's-eye with rings. When physicians take biopsies of these rings, they find the corkscrew-shaped bacterium that causes Lyme disease.

The Lyme disease rash does not necessarily occur at the site of the tick bite, and only about one-third of infected people will develop the bull's-eye. So any unusual or unexplained rash discovered after playing should be cause for suspicion. One of the difficulties in determining whether someone has Lyme disease is that it takes several weeks for the body's immune system to develop detectable antibodies. Even though the affected person may show symptoms, a blood test may not show the disease.

Early treatment with antibiotics should completely prevent Lyme disease. If untreated, the disease will progress from flu-like symptoms to inflammation of the knees and other large joints and then to full-blown arthritic and neurological symptoms that may be permanent. A new antibody test in the works may speed diagnosis and treatment. It helps determine whether antibiotics should be given orally or intravenously to treat the infection.

A Lyme disease vaccine is awaiting approval for marketing. When available, it would probably behoove golfers who play in high-risk areas to become vaccinated. The vaccine requires a series of three shots that will give you 80 percent immunity against Lyme disease 12 months later. People over age 65 get less protection from the vaccine, and booster shots may be needed to maintain immunity. Those who have been vaccinated should still take the usual precautions against the disease, such as using tick repellents (now included in some sunscreens), protective clothing, and rigorous tick surveillance and removal (see below).

Rocky Mountain Spotted Fever

Rocky Mountain spotted fever can be transmitted through the bite of the American dog tick. This tick is widely scattered throughout the country, but is found especially in the southeastern and central states. It is caused by rickettsia, microscopic organisms that are not bacteria, viruses, or fungi.

The classical sign for Rocky Mountain spotted fever is a small, spotted rash that occurs first on the palms of the hands or the soles of the feet and then spreads to other parts of the body. About two days after the tick bite, you will have a severe headache, a high fever, and severe muscle aches and weakness.

If the disease is not treated, it causes shaking chills, occasional abdominal pain, nausea, intense headaches, back stiffness, mental confusion, and finally unconsciousness. The later stages of the disease can damage the kidneys, liver, lungs, and blood.

Two blood tests measure antibodies that diagnose the infection. The second test looks for a large increase in antibodies 10 to 14 days after the illness begins. But there is a greater risk of more serious illness if antibiotic treatment is delayed. The antibiotics will usually cure Rocky Mountain spotted fever. But if the disease is not treated right away, you may have to be hospitalized to treat damage to internal organs.

Removing Ticks

If you are bitten by a tick, save the tick if possible in a container with a moistened paper towel in the refrigerator. If symptoms appear in 10 days to two weeks, the tick can be tested. Not all ticks are infected, but if it happens to be infected, that is a tremendous aid in knowing how to diagnose and treat the illness.

Ticks may be removed by grasping it as close to the head as possible with a tissue or pair of tweezers, then pulling it steadily until it releases itself from the body. Try to avoid direct contact with the tick. Forceps should not be used since they may crush the tick, pinch the body from the head, or crush the salivary glands. Additionally, do not use alcohol or a hot head of a match or pin or smother it with petroleum jelly. Any of these methods may cause the tick to salivate more and release more toxins into the body.

Once the tick is removed, use rubbing alcohol on the bitten area to minimize infection.

Precautions to Avoid Ticks

The best way to prevent tick-borne diseases is to avoid areas likely to contain ticks—for example, the woods on a golf course. Other precautions include the following:

- After a round, check your body for ticks, particularly on the scalp, armpits, groin, belt line, and back of the knees. These are areas where it may be difficult to see ticks. Check all exposed skin areas.

- Dress in light-colored clothing so you can see dark ticks. They may be as small as a pinhead.

- Wear socks that cover your ankles.

- Spray exposed skin with a tick repellent. Your clothing may also be protected with a special type of repellent.

- Tuck your pants into your socks before walking into tall rough or the woods.

- Shower promptly after playing using a washcloth to scrub away ticks.

- Wash your golf clothes or put them in high heat in the clothes dryer for 20 minutes, which will kill ticks.

⟦ E M E R G E N C Y ⟧ *Insect Bites and Bee Stings*

In the middle of a round one hot Florida day, I went to take a sip of soda and a yellow jacket sitting on the can's rim stung me. The inside of my upper lip swelled up, and it hurt like the dickens, but since our group was at the far end of the course, I just went on. At least the pain in my lip distracted me from the pain of my game.

Golfers are certainly exposed to insect bites. Swampy areas are breeding grounds for many insects, including mosquitoes. While annoying, most mosquito bites are not serious. Over-the-counter hydrocortisone cream is an effective treatment for most bites. I have found that a thick paste made of Adolph's Meat Tenderizer and water provides relief right away, particularly in northern Florida, where I play during the winter. When the paste dries out, wash it off and, if the stinging remains, apply it a second time.

If insects bother you, use an insect repellent before playing. There are two types of sprays, one for the skin and one for clothing, so check which one you are using before applying.

Bee stings are painful and can be fatal if the golfer is allergic to bees. Anyone with a history of allergy should carry an up-to-date Epi-pen, which contains epinephrine, in his or her golf bag. Injecting the drug will counteract an allergic reaction to a bee sting and prevent a severe immune system reaction, such as difficulty breathing. Someone in the golfer's group should know where the injectable drug is located and how to administer it. That's because golfers who are very sensitive and get rapid reactions may not be able to inject themselves.

RELIEVING RESPIRATORY PROBLEMS

Insects are not the only potential problems in the air for golfers. Allergens can cause problems such as allergies and asthma, which can affect your breathing and your game.

Allergies

Being an outdoor activity, golf raises the potential health problem of allergies. Golfers are at risk by their exposure to allergens, and the effects can be debilitating. Nasal allergies affect about 35 million Americans. The symptoms include sneezing, allergic rhinitis, itchy, tearing eyes, and swollen eyelids. If you have a cold that lasts longer than a week to a week and a half, the chances are you have allergies.

In people with allergies, the body mistakes allergens such as pollen, wood products, dust, and animal dander as enemies that need to be destroyed. When the body attacks these allergens, your nose becomes inflamed and swollen. This inflammation causes the nasal allergy symptoms.

One way to control allergies is to control their causes. This means avoiding or eliminating allergens that may trigger an allergy attack at home and at work.

Most people with allergies can control bothersome symptoms with drug therapy. For some, over-the-counter antihistamines, decongestants, or nasal sprays are effective. Others require prescription medications.

Several different types of medications are commonly used to treat allergies. Antihistamines offer relief by blocking the effects of the chemical histamine. Drowsiness is a common side effect. Decongestants work by shrinking the blood vessels in the nose. When decongestant sprays are used too often or for too long, symptoms can become worse, which is known as the rebound effect.

Anti-inflammatory nasal sprays work by reducing the inflammation or swelling in your nose. The most common side effects are nasal dryness or bleeding, or a burning sensation in your nose. Allergy shots may make your body less sensitive to certain allergens. Desensitization therapy involves injecting you with tiny amounts of these allergens so that your body learns to tolerate them.

Newer allergy medications do not cause drowsiness, but they do require a prescription. Two classes of these non-sedating antihistamine pills are available, with and without decongestants. Nasal sprays containing antihistamines or cortisone derivatives are also available. Decongestants open up the nasal passages, but the key ingredient, pseudoephedrine, may also keep you awake and may possibly cause heart palpitations. It may be necessary to experiment under the guidance of a physician to determine what is the most effective medication for you. For example, some people take a 12-hour medication with a decongestant during the day and another one without a decongestant at night.

Since allergy pills take about 1 hour to work, they should be taken before you start to play. Nasal sprays work within minutes, but you might need to take them again while on the course, so I recommend that golfers take the longer-acting oral allergy preparations.

Asthma

Asthma is a chronic, sometimes fatal disease in which allergens or irritants inflame airways in the lungs, which can close up suddenly and impair the ability to breathe. The most important substances or conditions that trigger asthma are allergies, upper respiratory infections, cigarette smoking, secondhand smoke, dust, cold air, exercise, aspirin, and air that contains particles, sulfur dioxide, ozone, or smog.

Most asthma seen among golfers is allergic. The pollen, grass, and weeds in the rough can trigger an asthma attack in golfers who are sensitive to these allergens. The intensity level of exercise in golf is not high enough to trigger exercise-induced asthma.

Everyone knows about the "noisy" part of asthma—the coughing, wheezing, and gasping for air. Yet most people are unfamiliar with the "quiet" part, the inflammation of the narrow tubes in the lungs that leads to the noisy symptoms. A whiff or two from an inhaler containing either bronchodilators or cromolyn sodium opens up swollen, irritated airways, and most asthma victims begin to breathe normally again in minutes. But an inhaler does not relieve the underlying inflammation, and the majority of asthma patients need to take additional anti-inflammatory drugs.

The first class of new asthma drugs in 20 years has recently won Food and Drug Administration (FDA) approval. These drugs inhibit the release of chemicals called leukotrienes that can cause asthmatics' lungs to become inflamed. Asthma patients who add these drugs to their regular medications have better control of the disease, with little or no side effects. Those who take these so-called leukotriene inhibitors breathe a little easier, sleep through the night, and drastically reduce their use of inhalant drops.

An experimental asthma drug, budesonide, will soon become the first powdered inhaled steroid. It has no taste, no smell, gives no sensation of going into the lungs, and has no side effects. Another boon for asthmatic golfers is a once-a-day nasal spray, Flonase, which provides 12-hour relief from the allergy symptoms that can trigger asthma.

Better medications and safer delivery systems make asthma a very treatable disease. Medications like leukotriene inhibitors and budesonide are like the sunscreens of asthma. By the time an asthma attack gets noisy, the damage has already been done by inflammation. Patients can use these new medications preventively before symptoms flare up.

Since all asthma drugs are available by prescription, a physician should help you decide which preparations would be best for you and oversee your treatment. Asthma should not prevent anyone from playing golf since it is very manageable with modern drugs.

Health Gadgets

Golfers are always looking for an edge. Like many sports, golf has become more competitive, even for casual players. A bunch of guys who may have once gone out for a good time on the weekend now end up playing all sorts of games within the game to keep things interesting. Losing a $5 Nassau may get a player's blood boiling. He will do anything, and try anything, to be able to beat his partners the next time out.

This eagerness to get better at almost any cost makes golfers vulnerable to health gadgets that may or may not have any value. Some are so far on the fringe of medicine that they smack of quackery. Others have some validity when used properly. Here's a look at what works, and what doesn't, among the current collection of health-related items marketed to golfers.

EXERCISE DEVICES

A tremendously wide variety of golf exercise devices are on the market, ranging from mere elastic tubing to very complicated mechanisms such as The Coach. While all of them probably will help with strength, and some of them with coordination, their costs generally far outweigh their benefits.

Strength Training

Everyone would like to hit the ball a mile, and that takes strength. Several golf devices promise to develop more power and improve your club head speed by working golf-specific muscles.

Some of these setups utilize plastic handles and elastic tubing. They provide a 20- to 30-minute, golf-specific workout that they claim adds yards to your drives and reduces the risks of injury. Using the elastic tubing against your own body for resistance, they help to build a more consistent golf swing by improving clubhead speed and control.

These devices, if used properly, do what they say, but for a price of up to $75, which usually includes an instruction video. For just a few dollars, you can buy simple elastic surgical tubing at any surgical supply house and accomplish basically the same result. Or try Therabands, which come in three resistance levels so that you can match them to your strength. These bands are available at sporting goods stores or gyms for about $13.

You can do the same exercise by tying one end of the surgical tubing or a fitness band to a doorknob and wrapping the other end around your left hand. Face the closed door and then turn and smoothly swing your left arm over your left shoulder as if you were making your backswing. Release and repeat. Do three sets of 10 repetitions. As you get stronger, shorten the elastic band or use a stronger Theraband.

The Coach, patented and endorsed by golf instructor David Leadbetter, is advertised as a golf fitness and strength training system. It is designed to help you shape and tone the muscles you need for a stronger, more consistent swing. The 10-minute workout teaches you to control your body rotation and hand position each time you swing.

This device takes you through your natural swing against resistance. The idea here is that you are exercising the muscles used during the swing so that the training is very specific. However, this type of machine is expensive, costing about $350. It does come with a teaching video and a 30-day returnable guarantee.

You can achieve much the same type of specific training by swinging a weighted club. You can buy either a weighted club for under $100 or a donut-type weight that you can put on your own club. These $5 donut weights are similar to the ones baseball players use in the on-deck circle to warm up before an at bat.

Be careful when you start using a weighted device. The sudden increase in weight of the clubhead can lead to injuries, such as pulled muscles, if you don't start slowly and gradually build up your clubhead speed. Work your way up to a full swing, but don't swing full out because the weight makes the club too heavy. Some golfers prefer a weighted club over the donut weight, which may get the club out of balance, but again consider the cost differential.

The very best way to increase your strength is with a planned strength training program using free weights or weight machines. A total body program will improve your strength much better than simply working the muscles of the golf swing. Balancing muscle groups is much more important to a good, athletic swing than developing specific muscles. For example, many chiropractors recommend that golfers practice reverse swinging, adding a reverse or opposite-handed practice swing before each regular practice swing, to balance out muscles and prevent back muscle strain. A golfer never allows the back muscles to coil and uncoil in two directions as a tennis player does in balancing forehand and backhand strokes.

One area that a golfer can always work on strengthening is the forearm. Inexpensive, hand-sized rubber grip balls bought at a surgical supply house, or hand putty found at drugstores, are excellent devices to increase your hand, wrist, and forearm strength. Keep a soft rubber ball in your jacket pocket and squeeze it whenever you have a few minutes to spare. Alternate hands to strengthen both sides.

Rehabilitation Devices

A beach ball–sized rubber ball used in rehabilitation of muscle injuries has gained tremendously popularity in the past few years. With the New York Giants football players, we use it as a tool to rehabilitate injuries to the back, hips, and legs. But you don't have to be hurt to make use of this ball. It is also an excellent device for increasing strength and flexibility in these body parts, as well as the abdomen.

These types of balls sell for about $40 at specialty sporting goods stores or by mail order. Some of them are inflatable; others come with handgrips. They may come with a step-by-step video and a wall chart to teach you easy exercises to build up strength and flexibility. But I suggest you get a good sports therapist or personal trainer to teach you how to use the ball. In a few sessions, the trainer can set up a 20-minute program that puts you through about a dozen strengthening and stretching exercises performed from sitting, standing, and prone positions.

In addition to strength and flexibility, the big ball's round surface requires you to develop stability, balance, and proprioception skills. Proprioception is the body's ability to recognize its position in space and to compensate for any imbalances. For example, try balancing on one foot for 30 seconds. Now close your eyes and do it again. You can feel the minute movements of your foot as you maintain your balance. Golf is a multidimensional sport with a changing center of gravity. Increasing your sense of balance and proprioception can only improve your game.

A recently introduced variation of the ball is a foam roller. This long, solid foam cylinder looks somewhat like a heavy punching bag lying on its side. Exercising on the roller is supposed to improve strength and increase motion in the back, particularly the upper back, which is hard to exercise. The roller also helps increase your sense of balance.

Back Bar

Imagine a dumbbell with firm balls on either side of the shaft instead of weights and you have an idea of what the Back Bar looks like. The Back Bar is billed as a self-massager. It works by stimulating acupressure points on the back to relieve muscle tension. You position it with a ball on either side of the spine in the muscle area, and then you roll up and down on it. The Back Bar can be used leaning against the wall or, for more pressure, lying on the floor. The symmetrical design and adjustable width help maintain the proper alignment on the golfer's spine.

Advertised as a means of relaxing tight, sore back muscles, it is one of the few products that does what it claims to do. It rapidly picks out tight, sore muscle spots, which can be massaged out by the rolling motion. Certainly, with muscular back problems so prevalent in golf, it is an aid to consider.

BRACES

Tennis Elbow Braces

Many golfers develop a form of tennis elbow (see chapter 8) from the swing. In addition to an exercise program, golfers can use a counterforce brace, just as tennis players do. These braces compress the extensor muscle in the arm and help relieve the elbow pain. One of the best is the Air Cast, an inflatable brace that not only can help control pain but prevent recurrences.

Ankle Braces

Air Cast also makes an inflatable ankle brace. Anyone who has recently sprained an ankle is at high risk for a recurrence until the ankle heals completely. Stepping into a divot hole or on a stone may result in your ankle turning over again, forcing you to go through another painful ankle rehabilitation (see chapter 11). The Air Cast brace, worn on top of your golf shoe and over the ankle, prevents the ankle from turning over. At the same time, it does not limit your ability to walk or swing the club.

Back Braces

Low-back pain is one of the most common problems among golfers. A variety of back bracing products are available to provide added back support and relieve muscle pain and stress. They sell for about $60 at golf specialty stores or through golf catalogs.

The Tourbelt looks like the back brace worn by construction workers or heavyweight lifters, except that it has an inflatable air bag in the backpack. A valve allows you to pump as much or as little air into the belt as needed. This varies the amount of support to your lower back. The belt can be worn under or over your golf clothes.

Solid S'port is a pair of elastic shorts with an adjustable, elastic, built-in, low-back support. Two tapered side pulls distribute support throughout the lower back. The manufacturer claims the fabric wicks away moisture, but it appears that it might be uncomfortable on a hot day.

Any back support is helpful for a golfer with low-back pain, but I do not recommend them to prevent back troubles. Constantly using back braces prevents back muscles from strengthening themselves because the support does all of the work, not the muscles. The muscles become dependent on the support and end up more prone to injury.

Hip Braces

Some professional golfers, including Raymond Floyd, have taken a page from other athletes and have begun to wear Lycra Power garments. These are the black, knee-length, rubberlike tights that professional football players have used for years to prevent muscle pulls. Raising the body temperature in the hip increases circulation to that area, which in turn increases the ability of muscles to stretch. Golfers, particularly older golfers, tend to have poor flexibility. It's difficult to stretch a cold muscle, and easy to stretch a warm one. So if you have a problem with your hips or with hamstring or buttocks muscles, wearing one of these garments under your golf pants will probably help.

PUTTING THE CART BEFORE THE HORSE

What's the best way to carry golf clubs? For my money, carrying the bag was the first and still is the best way, particularly in terms of getting the most exercise from a round of golf. Personally, I prefer a light canvas bag.

Pulling a cart behind also allows the golfer to walk and get some exercise, and still keeps the entire bag handy. When back problems flare up, as they are bound to, a pull cart may be the best solution. At least golfers still get to walk the course, and the bumpy ride of an electric cart can be murder on a bad back.

Another alternative is a double-strap golf bag. These bags are designed to relieve the strain of carrying a weighty bag on one shoulder. They first appeared among college golfers, who often walk 36 holes a day in tournaments.

Double-strap bags are based on the backpack principle—they balance the weight evenly by distributing the load over both shoulders. They are a more comfortable way to carry clubs, although the bag's weight still hangs off the spine, which may strain an already tender back.

Various designs are available, including a bag that can also be used as a single-strap bag for short distances, and those with foot stands and a flat bottom to place on the fairway. These bags may be more unwieldy to strap on and off. Make sure to use them properly to take full advantage of them and reduce shoulder pain and fatigue.

ELECTRIC WALKING GOLF CART

Maybe the ultimate in golf gadgets, electric walking carts are now available in several styles. These battery-powered carts haul the clubs for the golfer as he or she walks behind or next to his or her clubs. Some even have remote controls to send the clubs up ahead. The idea is that the golfer can enjoy walking the course, and they may even allow a better cardiovascular workout without the risk of joint strain from carrying or pulling the clubs on a cart. These motorized carts are also said to decrease fatigue because the golfer can walk unencumbered by clubs.

These fancy pull carts might have value for older golfers who are debilitated or those who have physical disabilities. However, most golfers who have trouble carrying a bag tend to ride in electric carts rather than walking the course.

Golfers who have had rotator cuff problems may also benefit from an electric walking cart. The position of the shoulder in pulling a cart may strain weak rotator cuff muscles, so a case can be made for the use of electric walking carts by able-bodied golfers with shoulder problems.

MAGNETS

In the early 1980s, I received a set of medicinal magnets to test. Since my wife, Gail, had a bad foot at the time, I put the hard, metal piece in her shoe. The salesman insisted it would help her, but it only made her foot feel worse. He also gave us a large metal magnet to put under our mattress to reduce my back pain. "You'll feel 100 percent better when you get out of bed," he said. The only thing it did was make me sleep with my head pointing north.

Medicinal magnets have been around for more than a dozen years with claims of relieving back pain, tendinitis, arthritis, and headaches. While several professional golfers claim wearing magnets helps relieve back pain and has allowed them to return to top form, there has been no medical evidence to show that magnets have any effect on golfers or any other athletes. In part because of endorsements by professional athletes, Americans now spend large sums on magnets for pain relief. The FDA has warned manufacturers and doctors about health claims for magnets.

The magnets theoretically stimulate nerve endings, which may help restore energy and increase blood circulation. The most popular ones are worn in a belt around the back, and are supposed to relieve lower back pain, sciatica, and muscle stiffness while increasing range of motion, which is essential for golfers. Other magnets inserted into insoles are designed for tired, aching feet, bunions, heel spurs, and arthritic conditions. A magnetic headband may relieve headache, migraines, and stress. And small half-dollar-size magnets can be taped to fingers and toes for arthritic fingers, bunions, and heel spur pain. Small, round magnets or credit-card-sized ones may also be strapped onto the neck, shoulder, or hips to supposedly relieve joint pain and stiffness. And a new golf shoe even has built-in magnets.

These small magnets marketed to golfers cannot be very potent. What kind of magnetic force can be generated by a finger-size magnet? The answer is very little.

There is something to be said for the idea of suggestibility. If a golfer thinks the magnet is going to work, it may well work some. Since there is no scientific evidence that magnets do anything, the only way to explain their reported ability to relieve pain is through the placebo effect. The placebo effect comes from controlled, scientific studies in which neither the doctor nor the patient know whether the medication the patient is taking is real or a dummy pill, known as a placebo. This type of study allows researchers to see whether a medication is really effective compared to the placebo, which theoretically should have no effect. In fact, medical studies show that if a doctor tells patients they are taking medicine, and gives them sugar pills, up to 40 percent of those patients will actually respond.

Although the exact source of a placebo's power is unknown, experts attribute it to mind-body interaction. They suspect it may be linked to the hope and belief that the substance will work. By taking it, the person may be aware that he is doing something to help control his condition. When people have a strong belief in a treatment, it changes their natural pain mediators and endorphins, the substances that boost the body's natural ability to tolerate pain.

Spontaneous relief of symptoms does occur, although rarely. If enough people use magnets for pain relief, a few will likely feel better.

Over the years, I have tried small magnets a number of times with New York Giants players because I had heard anecdotes of pain improvement from athletes and trainers. I have never found any improvement in symptoms or healing time over standard therapies. Since I have never heard a player say, "Yes, I feel better using magnets," I have discontinued using them.

There is a place in sports medicine for high-potency electromagnets to stimulate healing of hard-to-heal fractures. These magnets may be imbedded in a cast or strapped onto a limb. The high-energy electromagnetic field has been shown to improve healing in certain cases. These magnetic fields are much more potent than the small magnets sold to golfers.

Research is being done on the effects of magnets. One small pilot study conducted at the Baylor College of Medicine has raised some hope, but it is not the last word. In this study, 50 post-polio patients with chronic pain applied small devices directly over pain trigger points.

Some were active devices while others were inactive, sham devices. The patients and doctors treating them did not know which therapy the patients received.

Within about 45 minutes, the 29 patients who received an active magnet reported a significant reduction in pain compared to only a small reduction among the 21 who were treated with the sham magnet, and with no apparent side effects. The researchers concluded that new studies are needed to explore whether various strength magnets produce different degrees of benefit, how long the benefit lasts, whether the effect wears off after multiple applications, and the cost-effectiveness of pain management with magnets versus traditional drug therapy or physical therapy.

COPPER BRACELETS

I noticed that John, the young teaching pro from my local golf shop, had a copper bracelet around his wrist, so I asked him why he was wearing it. "It makes me feel better," he said. He had no joint pains or arthritis, or any other health problems, and scored regularly in the 70s. No wonder he felt good.

A wide variety of claims for improvement of arthritis, tendinitis, and assorted aches and pains have been made for thin copper bracelets worn around the wrist. The theory is that these conditions may be due to copper deficiency and that small amounts of copper are absorbed through the skin from the bracelet.

There has never been any reproducible scientific evidence that these bracelets are effective. Some people do seem to feel better, again possibly through suggestibility and the placebo effect. The results are usually temporary and do not actually treat the underlying problem. That is significant for people with progressive diseases, such as some types of arthritis. In general, arthritis patients need something that actually slows down the destruction of the joints. While it's good that a placebo makes you feel better, it has no long-term impact on disease progression.

Since we know that copper bracelets don't cause any harm, there is no reason for golfers who feel better to take the copper bracelets off. It may turn their skin green under the bracelet, but nothing else harmful will happen to them.

ALLOY BRACELETS

Another type of bracelet is made of a metal alloy and features a ball on either end of the wristband. It supposedly corrects an imbalance in positive and negative energy. I'm not quite sure what positive and negative energies are and how they get out of balance. Nowhere in medical literature or human physiology textbooks are these energies discussed. Eastern medicine touches on balancing out the chi (also spelled qi), or energy throughout the body, but I believe this is more metaphysics than medicine. I would place alloy bracelets in the realm of snake oil.

FOOD FADS

High-Energy Bars

High-energy bars are basically beefed-up granola bars. They contain about 200 calories, many more than simple granola bars. They do have an advantage over regular candy bars because they contain fructose rather than glucose. This avoids the sudden blood sugar elevation and then drop from a candy bar, which results in fatigue.

Energy bars are really designed for high-output workouts like mountain climbing, not golf. They probably are useful for golfers to overcome hunger in the course of playing 18 or more holes in one day, and will definitely help improve energy levels. The small packets are certainly easy to carry and quick, and quiet, to eat. Given the choice, an energy bar is more nutritious and better for your body than a candy bar. I still prefer eating a balanced diet and carrying a simple banana or a bagel in my bag for a snack. In fact, a recent study showed that bagels provide the same amount of carbohydrates as energy bars.

A specialized energy bar is being marketed specifically for golfers to increase concentration and energy and to provide calmness. The bar is a blend of herbs, vitamins, amino acids, and nutrients that supposedly gives golfers an advantage on the course.

Let's take a look at the main ingredients. The bar contains ginkgo biloba, a Chinese herb that is claimed to increase blood flow to the brain. Recent studies show that ginkgo may, indeed, slow the deterioration of Alzheimer's disease. But no one knows whether eating a small amount of ginkgo while playing golf improves concentration.

The amino acids included in the bar are found in dietary protein. Since the average American eats seven times as much daily protein as necessary, additional amino acids are simply surplus and would be excreted in the urine.

The additional protein for energy is ineffective because the body does not metabolize protein for energy, except during extreme starvation (and I don't mean that "starving" feeling in between nines). The carbohydrates will provide some extra energy, just as in any energy bar.

Vitamin B_{12} is added for calmness. The function of this vitamin is to produce hemoglobin. There is no evidence that it reduces stress, and it is poorly absorbed from the intestinal tract.

Vitamin E is a well-known antioxidant, but no one knows whether antioxidants have any role in performance enhancement.

Ginseng supposedly has stimulant properties similar to caffeine. Professional football, baseball, and basketball players have tried it in recent years. Basically, it has been discarded as a performance enhancer. And I wonder whether the added chamomile, which has a calming effect, counteracts the ginseng's stimulating effects.

SPORTS NUTRITION GELS

New to the sports nutrition scene, sports nutrition gels concentrate a high amount of energy into a gel pack that is swallowed, not chewed. These gels pack much more carbohydrates than the same amount of a sports drink. Chewing can be difficult during high-intensity exercise, such as running a marathon. But golf is not a high-intensity sport.

Stick with a sports drink and a high-energy snack, and drink water at all water stops along the course. These gels may even cause dehydration. The high concentration of carbohydrates greatly slows down absorption of fluid, and makes it harder for the body to get the water it needs, particularly on a hot, humid day.

SPORTS DRINKS

New sports drinks on the market developed just for golf work pretty much like other sports drinks. One drink originally created for the Norwegian cross-country ski team is a low-sugar, high-energy drink that purportedly avoids the peaks and valleys of other drinks because it is not sugar-based. It contains what amounts to the equivalent of a daily vitamin pill of vitamins and minerals, plus ginseng and guarana, two natural caffeine-like substances, and only 7 calories per serving. It comes in an effervescent tablet that you drop in water, so it's easy to take with you onto the golf course, and appears to be a useful alternative to other high-energy drinks.

Part Three

What to Know from Head to Toe

The Shoulders

Repetitively swinging a golf club eventually wears down the shoulders. While golf is not technically a throwing sport in which the entire arm goes over the head, the golfer's hands do go above the shoulder on both the backswing and the follow-through. This can lead to muscle weakness or problems with the rotator cuff, the four tiny muscles that control fine motion in the shoulder. These problems can lead to permanent scarring, bony growth in the shoulder joint, and the wearing out of the shoulder cartilage.

✚ ROUGH ROTATOR CUFF

As people age, the rotator cuff muscles get brittle and tend to tear. A rotator cuff tear is not uncommon in golf. Golfers generally do years of damage to the shoulders. Spurs may develop on the underside of the collarbone. This decreases the space for the rotator cuff, and the muscles start to fray without actually tearing. Older golfers are more prone to shoulder injuries because they already have damage to the rotator cuff and may have developed spurs.

Loose-jointed, younger golfers are most at risk for rotator cuff problems. They may develop tendinitis, or inflammation of the muscles, because the muscles become impinged at the top of the backswing and at the end of the follow-through. This particularly causes biceps tendinitis, or inflamed tendons where the biceps muscle attaches to the shoulder. In the rotated, upright position, the head of the shoulder may slide out of its socket slightly, causing pain in the back and top of the shoulder, inflammation, and biceps tendinitis, which causes pain down the side of the arm. It's usually a right-handed golfer's left shoulder that hurts because the left arm is moving with more force than the right arm during the follow-through. In baseball pitchers, the deceleration phase (stopping the arm after releasing the ball) causes most of the damage, and this is probably just as true for golfers.

HOW NOT TO TREAT ROTATOR CUFF PROBLEMS

Many doctors overlook the true problem—a loose shoulder joint—and treat shoulder tendinitis with anti-inflammatory agents or cortisone (steroid) injections. But the anti-inflammatory drugs soon wear off, and the next time you play a round, the tendon becomes inflamed again, the pain returns, and you need another injection or more anti-inflammatories. This may be good for the doctor, but is not good for you.

THE RIGHT TREATMENT FOR ROTATOR CUFF INJURIES

The best treatment is a series of exercises to strengthen the rotator cuff muscles to tighten the shoulder joint (see below). Most younger golfers will do fine if they work hard at shoulder exercises by themselves. Those that do not respond to a home exercise program may need to see a physical therapist to work with special exercise machines, or have the shoulder stabilized surgically.

Older golfers who continue to have shoulder pain should see a doctor to detect a possible bone spur or rotator cuff tear. A golfer who digs the club into hard ground can tear the rotator cuff muscles. This is marked by severe pain and loss of motion in the shoulder. The appropriate approach is similar: rehabilitate and re-strengthen the rotator cuff muscles. You may need surgery, either through an arthroscope, or an open procedure if rehabilitation is ineffective.

SHOULDER EXERCISES

Golfers can strengthen their rotator cuff muscles at home using light free weights. Do the following exercises 50 times a day or until fatigue sets in, using no more than 15-pound weights.

Arm Curl   *See page 31.*
Reverse Arm Curl   *See page 31.*
Front Lift (Palm Down)   *See page 28.*
Front Lift (Palm Up)   *See page 29.*
Lateral Lift   *See page 29.*
Bent-Over Lateral Lift   *See page 30.*
Bent-Over Chest Lift   *See page 30.*

✚ SHOULDER MUSCLE PULLS

A golfer's shoulders are subject to muscle pulls with the same mechanism as any area of the body: the muscle overcontracts or overstretches, causing muscle fibers to tear. The proper treatment is to rest the shoulder for a few days, followed by stretching (see stretching program, page 19) and strengthening exercises (see above). Make sure to warm up and then stretch the shoulder muscles before hitting any balls to prevent the muscle from pulling again.

A complex number of muscles around the shoulder can pull, and you may need to see a doctor if the muscle does not respond to home treatment. The doctor can diagnose which muscles are involved and possibly prescribe a physical therapy program specifically designed for those muscles.

The Back

Back injuries are the bane of a golfer's existence. They are the most common golf injury, mostly due to overuse. The rotational forces on the back from the golf swing are equal to more than eight times normal body weight, and can affect the back's bones, discs, ligaments, and muscles. The amateur golfer who plays sporadically without proper warm-up and with poor swing mechanics can suffer muscle strains, disc problems, a cracked back, and arthritis.

The golf swing requires constant rotation of the hips and trunk muscles, with comparatively little flexing and extending of the hip muscles. As a result, the muscles that flex and extend the hips become weaker and tighter over time, creating an imbalance that can lead to low-back pain. Other common causes of low-back pain are weak abdominal muscles and frequent walking up and down hills on the course.

CLASSIC VERSUS MODERN SWING

The golf swing itself can lead to back problems. In the Classic swing, the backswing follows a flat swing plane, with hips rotating almost as much as the shoulders. On the follow-through, the golfer's body ends up in a straight up-and-down "I" position.

The Modern swing relies on a lightly coiled body to store power for maximum clubhead speed at impact. This swing ends with the golfer's body in a reverse "C" position with hands high and right shoulder lower than the left shoulder. It's more powerful, but much more stressful on the back.

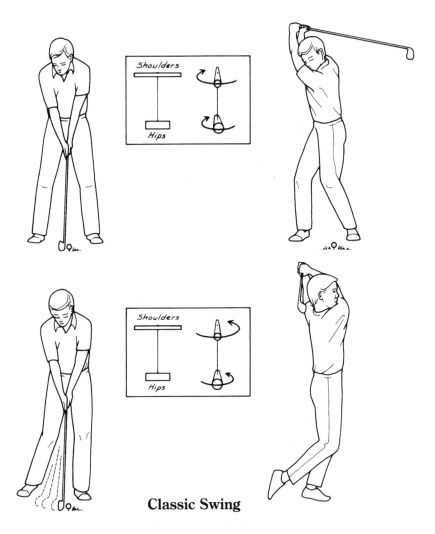

Classic Swing

If you are prone to back problems, make sure you have the proper swing mechanics to prevent problems by consulting with a golf professional. If you have chronic back problems, learning the Classic swing will often be all you need for relief.

✚ MUSCLE STRAINS

Probably 95 percent of lower back injuries are due to muscle strains. The big muscles of the back, the strongest muscles in the body, become hard

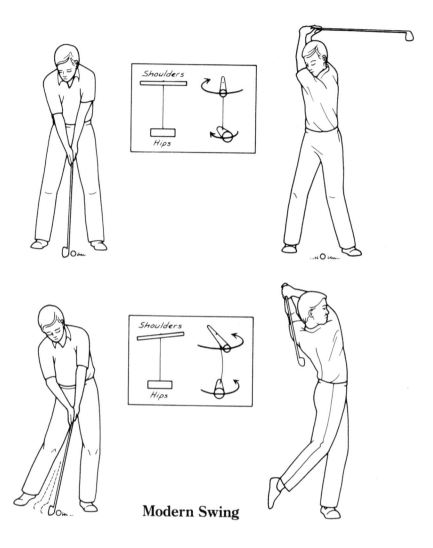

Modern Swing

and tender to touch when strained, with pain on either side of the spine. Some strains can become acute muscle pulls. Significant muscle spasms may begin gradually with periods of severe pain, and then relief. These pains are not associated with sciatica or referred pain down the leg, which can occur later when muscles pull on nerve roots on the spine.

Back strains are relieved by rest and anti-inflammatory agents. Golfers should ice sore muscles, 20 minutes on, 20 minutes off, take a few days off from golf, and use anti-inflammatories to relieve pain. When you feel better, a back-stretching program can lengthen muscles so that they don't tighten down and shorten, or they will pull again. If the pain becomes persistent, see a doctor.

Year-round trunk-strengthening exercises and warming up and stretching before playing can help prevent back muscle strains.

MD DISC PROBLEMS

Disc problems are quite rare among golfers, but are easy to discern—if you hear a snap or pop in your back as you swing, you know you are in trouble. One to two days later, leg pain may develop. The pain will appear where a disc has ruptured. A lower back disc will cause sciatic pain down the leg; a disc above this causes pain down the front of the leg. The leg pain is usually worse than the back pain.

Anything that increases pressure in the spinal column—sitting, coughing, or sneezing—will exacerbate the pain. An at-home test helps golfers know if the problem is a disc. Have someone raise your leg with the knee locked to the point of onset of pain. Then have him or her pull the foot up toward the knee. An increase in pain is a good indication of a disc problem.

Anyone with these symptoms needs to see a doctor. The pain usually responds to rest, pain relief with medications, and stopping playing. Once the acute symptoms resolve and leg pain goes away, a rehabilitation program, led by a physical therapist, for the back and affected leg areas is recommended. Only a small percentage of golfers will require surgical repair. Simple surgery has the golfer up and walking within a day or two, but a return to golf could take several months.

MD A CRACKED BACK

A cracked back, or spondylolysis, is a fracture of the narrow part of a vertebra connecting the front and back halves. Some people are born with the two parts of the vertebra unfused. Golfers who have increased narrowing in the backbone may crack their back from a strong swing or a fall. This is much more common in young golfers. Older golfers are not immune from this back pain, which may eventually develop over the years when the fractured bone slips.

The golfer will feel pain and tenderness right over the backbone. Arching the back makes it worse. Standing on one leg and arching the back gives a good indication if the cause is spondylolysis. Back extension exercises will exacerbate the pain.

You need to stop playing until the pain quiets down. If at-home tests suggest this condition, see a doctor. Specialized X rays and possibly a bone scan are needed to make the diagnosis. Early diagnosis is important because it can progress to spondylolythesis, a more serious condition in which the spinal cord is compressed, and which can possibly lead to paralysis. If the golfer continues to have symptoms, an X ray every six months may be necessary to make sure the backbone has not slipped any further.

If you have signs of a cracked back, switch to the Classic swing, which does not arch the back. This condition responds to trunk-strengthening exercises. All other activities that put weight on the spine, such as lifting heavy objects, should be avoided. For persistent pain, a back brace may help.

✚ ARTHRITIS ACHES

Arthritis of the back joints is usually the result of aging. This is commonly caused by the pressure of the rotatory motion of golf, and wear and tear on the joints between the vertebrae. It usually starts with vague aches and pains in one spot in the spine. Eventually it becomes a deep, aching pain and radiates to the whole lower back area, buttocks, and upper thighs.

Arthritis will not get better if the golfer keeps playing. Generally, the pain is exacerbated by walking and relieved by sitting, which is the opposite of disc pain. Treatment is to limit activity, take anti-inflammatory agents, and to wear a back brace. However, while a brace provides relief, the back muscles lose strength. A golfer should be careful not to weaken back muscles, and should begin doing back exercises as the symptoms subside. An increased warm-up time and better swing mechanics are recommended on your return to golf.

If the pain does not disappear within a few weeks, see a doctor.

PREVENTING BACK PROBLEMS

A strong back is the basic prevention for back problems. Since muscle weakness causes most back injuries, increased strength will prevent most injuries.

Back and sports medicine doctors have traditionally prescribed exercises to strengthen the flexor muscles of the back. These muscles pull the back forward and down. But gravity naturally pulls the body in that direction. To lift your trunk into an erect position, you must use the extensor muscles. So once you can do early flexion exercises, you must concentrate on extension exercises.

A Back-Strengthening Program

Back pain manifests itself in different ways in different people, and there are many different types of treatment. I prefer ice treatments for 20 to 30 minutes at a time, two to three times a day, for as long as the back is sore. I only prescribe heat once the back has healed and to loosen it up before playing.

Bed rest used to be the standard advice, but now we know that more than a few days of rest only weakens your muscles and can be disabling. You need to get out of bed as soon as possible. Consider surgery only as a last resort.

Golfers with back problems will likely wind up on a regimen of daily stretching and strengthening exercises. These reconditioning exercises are designed to support the back, especially the abdominal muscles; stretch overly tight muscles and ligaments in the back; and reduce defects in posture that strain the back. Strong, flexible muscles around the lower back and abdomen stabilize the spine and protect it from injury.

Back-Stretching Exercises

The following exercises can be done at home to stretch the flexor and extensor muscles. For an acutely injured back, start with flexion exercises. As you become more comfortable and your back muscles begin to lengthen, you can start extension exercises.

Flexion Exercises

Forehead-to-Knee Stretch   *See page 15.*
Toe Touch with Rotation   *See page 16.*
Hurdler Stretch (Standing)   *See page 11.*
Knee Pull   *See page 19.*
Pelvic Tilt   *See page 26.*
Abdominal Crunch   *See page 25.*

Extension Exercises

Back Extension   *See page 26.*
Hip Extension   *See page 13.*

Reverse Sit-Up

This exercise in-
volves working with
a partner, who will
hold your legs
down. Lie on your
stomach on a table,
with only your legs and pelvis on the table.
Have your partner hold your ankles while
you bend at the waist off the edge until
your forehead is pointing to the floor. Then
slowly lift your upper body until it is hori-
zontal again. Do five repetitions and add
two at a time as this becomes easier. This
should only be started when the back is
pain free and the back extension and hip
extension exercises are easy to do.

Back-Strengthening Exercises

To strengthen your lower back, do back extension exercises regularly, in
particular the Reverse Sit-Up, and also do abdominal muscle exercises to
help take the pressure off the back muscles.

If you use your large trunk muscles when hitting the ball, you can
generate much more power than you can with the smaller muscles of the
arms and shoulders. Following are three trunk exercises you can do to
strengthen the trunk muscles.

Bent-Waist Rotation   *See page 17.*

Runner

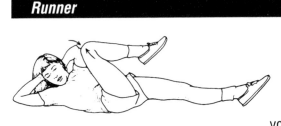

This exercise strengthens the rotator muscles on the sides of the stomach. Lie on your back, hands behind your head. Raise your right knee toward your chest and keep your left leg straight. Now touch your left elbow to your right knee, and then repeat with the opposite leg and elbow until your muscles are exhausted.

Thigh Thinner

This is basically a straight leg lift. Lie on your side and lift one leg up. Do five sets, with 10 to 20 repetitions per set. Repeat with the other leg.

PREVENTING BACK STRAIN

While some doctors recommend that back pain sufferers avoid sports that put severe stress on the back, a back problem should not doom a golfer to a life without the links. If you take precautions, you can play pain-free golf.

Golfers should beware of the torsion placed on the back during the swing. The sideways tilting of the body during the swing contributes to low-back pain. Many golfers with right-side, low-back pain experience more pain during the impact of the golf ball through the follow-through phase of their swings. So toning up the abdominal muscles is especially important. Also, remember to bend at the knees, not the waist, when placing a tee in the ground and when lining up a putt. Instead of hunching over the ball, adjust your stance, or your club length, so you will be upright when you follow through on your swing. This may eliminate your back pain.

You are at risk of throwing out your back from golf because of all of the twisting and turning. Take it easy at the start of the season, and always ease muscles in and out of activity with warm-up and stretching. If you are out of shape, don't push yourself beyond your range of motion.

The Elbow

Hideo, a Japanese man in his 40s, came to see me, holding his elbow bent in front of him. "What happened to your elbow?" I asked. "I learned to play golf. I hit very hard, but I didn't hit the ball. I hit the ground." I put him into a physical therapy program, but he had damaged his elbow so much that he needed cortisone injections. It took eight weeks—and a series of golf lessons—before he was back on the course.

The elbow is a common source of misery for golfers. The elbow is actually three separate joints, consisting of the junction of the two bones of the forearm and the junction of each of these bones with the humerus, the bone of the upper arm. These three joints allow the elbow to bend and straighten as well as to rotate.

An elbow injury can also be caused by wrist problems. The muscles that control the wrist originate from the elbow's bones. So some problems that arise from excessive wrist strain cause pain in the elbow rather than the wrist.

✚ TENDER TENDONS

Elbow pain is usually the result of a sudden impact with the ground when the golfer creates a divot. Hitting into the ground, a tree root, or another immovable object can cause acute trauma to elbow tendons, most commonly those in the right arm. These tendons may even tear partially or become detached from the bone.

Tendon damage may also be caused by a weak grip, when your right hand is turned too far to the right when holding the club. This causes excessive rotation of the forearms during the downswing and accentuates the load on the inside of the right elbow.

Injuries to elbow tendons, either acute or through overuse, can cause scarring and reduce the tendon's resistance to injury. A tennis player who had tennis elbow and plays golf is more likely to have chronic elbow pain.

The treatment for tender tendons is rest to allow the tendons to heal, followed by an elbow-strengthening program (see below). Golfers who return too soon will likely reinjure the elbow tendon, even if they hit the ball well.

✚ GOLFER'S ELBOW

The most common type of elbow pain is called golfer's elbow. Traditionally, doctors believed that golfers only had pain on the outside of the left (nondominant) elbow, and dubbed this golfer's elbow to differentiate it from pain on the inside of the right (dominant) elbow, called tennis elbow. But there seems to be an equal number of problems on both sides of the elbows of golfers.

A right-handed golfer normally feels pain in the left elbow. Pulling the club through the swing with the left wrist causes irritation in the left elbow. So a right-handed golfer who feels pain in the right arm or wrist is doing something terribly wrong during the swing.

Golfer's elbow is an inflammation of the muscles of the forearm and the tendon that connects the muscles to the bones in the elbow. These muscles are used to bend the wrist backward and to turn the palm face up. When the muscles and tendon become inflamed from overuse, you feel pain on the outside of the elbow. The pain is worse when you try to lift things with your palm facing down, so you may have trouble picking up a coffee cup or taking a quart of milk out of the refrigerator.

This injury also causes pain when you rotate your hand in a counter-clockwise direction. You also will feel pain when you clench or squeeze something, such as when you hold a golf club.

Treatment for golfer's elbow is the same as for tennis elbow—rest and anti-inflammatory agents, followed by physical therapy and a wrist-strengthening program. Cortisone injections are only used when this fails. On rare occasions, surgery is necessary to reattach tendons to bone. If elbow pain is very severe, or if it persists for more than a few weeks and prevents playing, see a doctor.

THE AGING ELBOW

Increased frequency of play can become a problem in the 35- to 55-year-old group of golfers. Two to three rounds a week seems to be the threshold. The more a golfer plays, the more likely the chance of elbow pain. So if you start to feel elbow pain, you may want to cut back your playing and practicing time. It does no good to beat bucket after bucket of balls instead of playing—the elbow will be stressed whether you are at the range or on the course.

SWING MECHANICS

Deviating from a neutral swing to one that is too flat or too steep requires a correction of the hands at impact to hit the ball squarely. This correction leads to an increase in elbow strain. If you have sudden elbow pain and have not had an acute injury—that is, jarred the elbow with a mishit—you may have developed a mechanical problem in your swing. Have your local pro check out your swing and make any necessary corrections.

CONDITIONING

Conditioning is important to prevent elbow pain. Stronger muscles can handle more stress without injury. Elbow-strengthening exercises allow the tendons to absorb more shock, and the golfer is less likely to have in-flammation.

Once your elbow has become inflamed, everyday activities are enough to keep it irritated. Giving up your weekly golf game to rest your elbow is not enough to solve the problem. Treating golfer's elbow requires an exercise program to increase the strength and flexibility of the forearm muscles and tendon. Once they are strong enough to withstand the stress of playing, the pain will go away and should not return.

Forearm-Strengthening Exercises

Do the Elbow and Wrist strengthening exercises found in chapter 1, in-cluding Arm Curl (page 31), Reverse Arm Curl (page 31), Wrist Curl (page 32), Reverse Wrist Curl (page 32), Roll-Up (page 33), and Unbal-anced Wrist Rotation (page 32). Start with light weights (5 pounds for men, 2.5 pounds for women) and gradually increase the weight as your strength improves. Do 50 repetitions of each exercise or until the mus-cles are exhausted.

Elbow Flexibility Exercises

An increase in muscle and tendon flexibility can also help prevent elbow pain. When you start an elbow-strengthening program, you may feel some pain because you are overloading the elbow to make it stronger. The Elbow Stretch (Palm Up) on page 20 and the Elbow Stretch (Palm Down) on page 20 in chapter 1 are flexibility exercises that stretch the elbow and help relieve this pain.

BETTER EQUIPMENT

The golfer with chronic elbow pain may need to change clubs to reduce the shock transmitted to the elbow. Oversize heads found in newer woods increase the size of the sweet spot, as do the cavity back/perimeter weighted irons, and reduce stress on the elbow. Graphite shafts, with varying degrees of flexibility compared to metal shafts, may help lessen the effects to the elbow, particularly from mishits. If you take large divots or often strike the ground hard, consider buying golf clubs that absorb or dampen vibrations.

The Wrist and Hand

Wrist injuries are quite common among golfers, particularly amateurs, with more than one-third of all golf injuries found in the wrists and hands. With all of the turning of the hips and shoulders to increase the speed of the swing, the impact still goes through the wrists and hands, setting them up for injury.

➕ THUMB TENDINITIS

Inflammation in the extensor tendon, which extends the thumb, can lead to pain in the side of the wrist directly below the base of the thumb. The cause of the thumb tendinitis is the pressure of the club on the thumb at the top of the backswing. It may also be due to "casting," where the wrists are uncocked at the top of the downswing instead of at impact. This move causes an off-plane swing with an outside to inside motion, which causes a slice or pull, and puts excessive strain on the thumb side of the wrist.

The thumb will feel tender and swell up. So will the side of the wrist behind the thumb. Occasionally, the tendon will squeak as the thumb is moved, particularly when the golfer moves the thumb toward the little finger.

Treatment is rest, ice, and anti-inflammatory agents. The thumb may need to be splinted to immobilize it. In severe cases, a cortisone injection will relieve the pain. If all else fails, surgery can open the tendon sheath to give the tendon more room to move.

To prevent thumb tendinitis, you need to strengthen the forearm and fingers. Do the Ball Squeezing exercise on page 33 to the point of fatigue as many times a day as you can to improve your grip strength.

You can also improve the movement of your fingers by doing exercises with a rubber band. The large rubber bands used by grocery stores on broccoli or celery provide about the right amount of resistance.

Thumb and Fingers Flex

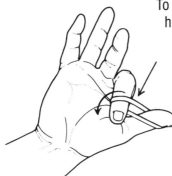

To make your fingers stronger in flexing, hook a rubber band around the thumb and one finger, and try to close the finger to the palm. Hold for 5 seconds. Do the same exercise with each of the fingers of the hand.

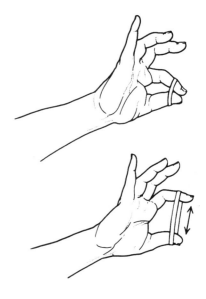

Thumb and Fingers Stretch

With your palm facing you, hook a rubber band around the thumb and the index finger, and stretch the rubber band between the fingers. Hold for about 1 second and repeat until fatigued. Then move the rubber band to each of your other fingers and stretch them individually against the thumb.

Adjacent Fingers Stretch

Put a rubber band across two adjacent fingers and spread them apart, holding for 5 seconds. Stretch each combination of adjacent fingers in the hand.

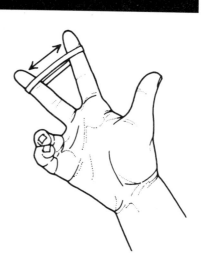

✚ WRIST IMPINGEMENT

If you overcock your left wrist at the top of the backswing, the bone at the base of the left thumb can bang into the bone where the thumb connects to the wrist. Constantly overcocking the wrist to the inside will cause pain in the depression between the base of the thumb and the wrist. In fact, you will feel pain in that area every time you cock your wrist, whether on or off the course.

You must stop playing until the pain quiets down. In the meantime, ice the tender area and take anti-inflammatory agents to ease the pain. To prevent this injury, do not overcock your wrist and the bones will not bang into each other. If you feel this pain, take a lesson to correct the position of the left wrist at the top of the backswing.

MD TENDON SHEATH RUPTURE

This is an injury that can occur when the club strikes the ground or a tree root and stops suddenly. Usually the golfer feels sudden, severe pain in the back of the left (nondominant) wrist. This is a major injury and requires casting of the wrist by a doctor. A golfer whose clubhead speed seems to be decelerating and has severe pain in the back of the wrist should see a doctor immediately.

MD TRIGGER FINGER

Trigger finger is a thickening of the tendon sheaths in the palm with a locking of the finger in a bent position. It can be pulled straight out with the other hand and the tendon will snap into place. This is due to gripping the club with the left hand turned over to the right. On impact with the ball or the ground, the club jars the tendon sheath. It is most common in the third or fourth fingers.

Treatment is a cortisone injection, which reduces inflammation in the tendon sheath. If this fails, the tendon sheath can be opened surgically to allow free motion of the finger. Replacing grips frequently or possibly switching to larger grips may soften the impact and help prevent the injury.

✚ CARPAL TUNNEL SYNDROME

Carpel tunnel syndrome is the all-too-common damage done by repetitively grasping and flexing the hand. This syndrome leads to pain, numbness, or even loss of strength in the third and fourth fingers. It can extend up into the forearm and down into the hand.

The treatment is to rest and apply ice to the affected wrist. If that does not work, then anti-inflammatory agents may help. If the pain persists, see a doctor. A cortisone injection usually provides relief. Surgery to cut the ligament at the bottom of the wrist is a last resort to relieve the pressure. Again, larger grips may help so that the hands do not squeeze the club as tightly.

To avoid carpal tunnel syndrome, try the following stretching exercises:

Fingertip Pull

Rest one forearm on a table, and then grasp the fingertips of that hand and pull back gently. Hold for 5 seconds. Repeat with the fingers of the other hand.

Palm Press

Press your palm flat on a table, as if doing a push-up, and lean forward to stretch the forearm muscles and wrist. Hold for 5 seconds.

🄼🄳 BROKEN HAND

A broken hand is more common in tennis than golf. The bone in the heel of the palm below the little finger has a slender hook where a tendon attaches. The butt of the club can hit this hook on a "fat" shot or on striking the ball on hard ground, causing sudden, intense pain.

Since this is a fracture, the hand needs to be surgically repaired. Pain can be evoked by flexing the fourth and fifth fingers against resistance.

The golfer may also feel chronic, less severe pain due to recurrent bruising of the hook without breaking the bone. The golfer should get his clubs refitted so that the butt of the shaft does not sit directly over the hook in the fleshy part of the hand.

✚ BLISTERS AND CALLUSES

Many golfers suffer blisters and calluses on their hands and fingers from gripping the club, particularly early in the golf season. Blisters form on skin that is damaged by friction and burns. Sweat makes your skin sticky, and the friction between your hands and the club can cause blisters.

I prefer to treat blisters by leaving them alone and letting them heal. New skin forms under the blister, and the fluid in the blister gradually becomes absorbed. Eventually, the outer layer of skin sloughs off. If a blister breaks or becomes damaged by further friction, then use an antibiotic ointment and dressing. If it becomes infected, see a physician.

Calluses are areas of skin that have thickened because of constant pressure. The pressure causes the tissues underneath the callus to become tender. If the callus becomes bothersome, you can soften it with a cream or ointment and rub away dead skin with a pumice stone. If this does not help, a physician can trim the callus surgically or chemically.

To prevent these uncomfortable annoyances, you need to find out what is causing them. You may not be holding the club properly, or you may need new grips.

PREVENTING HAND INJURIES

There's not much you can do to prevent hand injuries since most of them are caused by accidents. You can use golf gloves, on both hands if necessary, to prevent minor problems such as blisters and calluses.

Strong fingers are important in almost every sport. They are especially important in golf for holding the club lightly but securely. Following is one simple finger exercise.

Finger Stretch

Hold your hands out in front of you, palms facing each other and fingers straight up. Bend fingers down and squeeze them as tightly as you can. Hold for 5 seconds and then release. Repeat five times a day for stronger fingers and a better grip.

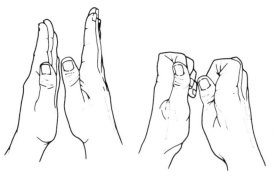

10

The Knee

On a public course on Long Island, I met Paul, a 40-year-old fisherman, who played in knee-high rubber boots. "I've had surgery on both knees for torn cartilage, and my doctor told me I might tear them up again if I wore golf shoes," he said before we teed off. At the turn, Paul was only two over par, and I wondered out loud whether I could buy a pair of rubber fishing boots in the pro shop—anything to help my game.

While the knee is not as stressed in golf as in many other sports, it does suffer most commonly from overuse injuries caused by the rotation of the knee back and forth during the golf swing. A golfer can aggravate soreness under the knee—a condition known as runner's knee—by walking the course, particularly if the terrain is hilly. Knees that have had cartilage removed do not do well with the strains of golf. And many older people turn to golf as a less strenuous exercise, but the wear and tear on the knee can exacerbate arthritic symptoms.

✚ SPRAINED KNEE

Acute injuries are rare in golf and usually occur from falling or slipping. This may sprain or even tear knee ligaments. The knee will swell up, and you will have trouble walking on that leg.

A knee sprain is an injury to a knee ligament. The sprain may vary in severity from a slight stretch to a complete tear of the ligament. A mild, or grade 1, sprain simply stretches the ligament and causes pain and swelling. A moderate, or grade 2, sprain partially tears the ligament and is much more disabling. A severe, or grade 3, sprain is a complete rupture and often needs surgical repair. Most golfers will suffer mild sprains.

The immediate treatment for a sprained knee is to rest the knee while it aches and ice it intermittently several times a day, and then wrap it in an elastic bandage in between icing and keep it elevated as much as possible.

Knee Sprain Rehab

A mild sprain will respond to an early rehabilitation program using a stationary bicycle and leg extension and leg curl exercises. Begin by riding a stationary bicycle for 20 minutes. Keep the seat high so that your range of motion is minimal. Don't put any drag on the bike; you are simply interested in moving the knee. Once you can pedal easily, lower the seat gradually so that you increase the bend in your knee each day until you get back your full range of motion.

Do Leg Extension (see page 27) and Leg Curl (see page 26) exercises. Once you lift the weight, hold it for 3 seconds and then very slowly lower the weight. Concentrate on the slow movement down, which is the most important part of the lift. Muscle contraction against weight while the muscle is lengthened builds the most strength.

The purpose of these exercises is to strengthen the quadriceps muscle in the front of the thigh (Leg Extension) and the hamstring muscles in the back of the thigh (Leg Curls). These muscles control the knee and must be restrengthened.

Anything more severe than a minimal knee sprain should be seen by a physician. A physician may prescribe a rehabilitation program that consists of sophisticated strengthening exercises, bracing, and physical therapy.

MD TORN CARTILAGE

The grinding action of the knee as it rotates can damage cartilage. This is rare for golfers, but can happen over time.

If you tear cartilage, you will feel pain and see swelling in the knee. You may hear a clicking sound inside the knee when you move it. This is the bone riding over the torn part of the cartilage. When you twist your knee, the knee may slip and buckle and even cause you to fall.

Most cartilage tears do not heal by themselves. Cartilage has a poor blood supply except at the outer rim, so about 90 percent of cartilage tears have no ability to heal. The torn piece of cartilage has to be cut out. The most common way is to shave down the ragged edges of the tear with tiny instruments manipulated through an arthroscope. Arthroscopic surgery is minor surgery in an expert's hands.

If the tear is at the outer edge of the cartilage, or if it is small, it may heal. Healing requires a rehabilitation program similar to that described for sprained knees to re-strengthen the muscles around the knee. Follow the rehabilitation program and you can usually return to full activity within 3 to 4 weeks.

Many patients suffering from knee injuries enjoy golf as a hobby. But golfers recovering from knee surgery should cool their desire for a quick return to the golf course, according to Ohio State University researchers. They found that the forces acting on a golfer's knees during the downswing of a golf club have the same impact as running in a straight line and abruptly turning 90° left or right. So getting out to the green too quickly after surgery could prove hazardous to a healing knee.

If a knee injury affects your dominant leg—for example, the right leg of a right-handed golfer—it takes about 2 months for that knee to get back to normal. The nondominant leg usually takes 3 months to heal.

✚ SORE KNEES

Many golfers have sore knees from playing too much. Here's how to prevent the pain:

- Decrease frequency of play. Find a frequency that allows enough satisfaction without increasing symptoms.

- Use short irons only. There is less strain on the knees with the short irons than with the long irons and woods. While this may increase a golfer's score, it permits continued play. Or switch to shorter par 3 or executive courses at least some of the time.

- Take golf lessons. A change in technique may enable the golfer to reduce strain on the knee. The swing should have equal distribution of weight on both feet. Many golf schools teach players to sway to reduce back problems, but this increases the strain on the left knee for right-handed golfers. Hitting off the back foot increases strain on the right knee.

- Use an upright stance. Golfers with sore knees should use a more upright stance with less knee flex. More upper body flexibility reduces knee strain. Splaying the feet out slightly may also reduce pressure on the knees.

- Choose the right clubs. Longer, lighter, more flexible clubs with graphite shafts reduce the overall effort of the golf swing and stress on the knees.

- Switch to soft spikes. Regular metal golf spikes fix the foot into the ground to add power to the swing, but they increase the torsion on the knee. Use new spikeless shoes with soft, rubber spikes, old shoes with worn down spikes, or new shoes with spikes filed down about 50 percent.

RUNNER'S KNEE

The most common overuse injury to the knee, and the most common cause of knee pain, is runner's knees, known medically as chondromalacia patella or patello-femoral syndrome. This is caused by misalignment of the kneecap in its groove. The kneecap normally goes up and down in the groove as the knee flexes and straightens. If the kneecap is misaligned, it will pull off to one side and rub on the side of the groove. This causes both the cartilage on the side of the groove and the cartilage on the back of the kneecap to wear out. On occasion, fluid builds up and causes swelling in the knee.

As a result, you will experience pain around the back of the kneecap or in the back of the knee after playing a round. You also will have difficulty going up and down the clubhouse stairs. Golfers can try to play flatter courses or ride carts. However, riding destroys most of the exercise benefits to the heart.

The basis of the problem is not the knee but the foot. An inward roll of the foot and ankle causes the shinbone to rotate to the inside, which turns the knee to the inside as well. The kneecap ends up sliding at an angle instead of straight up and down.

Treatment involves correcting the foot strike by propping up the foot with an arch or orthotic device inside the golf shoe. This prevents excessive pronation and keeps the knee in alignment. Start with a commercial arch support and progress to a handmade orthotic if necessary for pain relief.

You can also do a special exercise to strengthen the inner side of the quadriceps muscle. Normally, a full leg extension strengthens the quadriceps. However, as the quadriceps contracts, it pulls the kneecap back into the groove and grinds it against the side as you lift your leg. If you have runner's knee, this full extension worsens the symptoms.

You can get around this. The inner side of the quadriceps muscle comes into play only in the last 30 degrees, or 6 to 8 inches, of a full leg extension. At this point the kneecap is up out of the groove. The idea is to work the quadriceps only within these last 6 to 8 inches of the lift, as described in the 30-Degree Leg Extension.

30-Degree Leg Extension

To limit the Leg Extension, put something under your foot so that your heel can come down only 6 to 8 inches after your leg is fully extended. For example, sit on a kitchen table or a desk and attach ankle weights or hang a tote bag filled with free weights from your ankle. Then take a chair or stool and pile books on it a height of 6 to 8 inches below your heel when your leg is fully extended. As you come down, your heel will hit the books and stop your knee from bending.

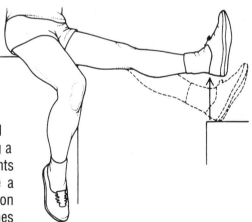

If you are exercising on a bench with a leg machine, put a cinder block or box under the bar so that your leg stops 6 to 8 inches below full extension.

If you are exercising on a weight machine, first lift the stack of weights to full extension. Then have someone else put a second pin into the stack so that when the weights come down 6 to 8 inches, the pin blocks them from going any further.

Do five sets of 10 repetitions with enough weight so that your muscle is exhausted during the last set. When the exercise gets easy, increase the weight. Do this once a day every day until you are pain-free, then do the exercise two or three times a week to keep the quadriceps muscle strong.

Bending the knee more than 30 degrees will cause symptoms to flare up, so any kind of bent-leg exercise, such as leg presses or squats, is bad. When riding a stationary bicycle, keep the seat high so that you bend your knee as little as possible. Use a step machine that allows you to adjust the height of the step and use a short step.

✚ ARTHRITIS PAINS

Golfers with arthritis in the knee should take their medication before and after playing to reduce swelling. If need be, ride a cart and walk as much as is comfortable in between shots to get some aerobic benefit.

Osteoarthritis is the wear-and-tear degeneration of the knee. Spurs of bone form along the edges of the knee joint and wear down the cartilage. Bowlegged people may develop severe osteoarthritis of the knee because the bowing causes increased pressure of the inner part of the tibia (shinbone) against the knee joint. This wears out the inner cartilage and causes bone to grate on bone, leading to arthritis.

Bone spurs or pieces of worn-down cartilage can break off and float around in the knee. This causes pain during golf and swelling of the joint. Anti-inflammatory agents will help ease the pain. If an X ray reveals that you have a large amount of debris in the knee, arthroscopic surgery can clean out the joint and provide relief for up to a few years. Then your knee may need to be cleaned out again.

If the pain becomes so severe that it interferes with your game, the knee may have to be replaced with an artificial joint.

11

The Lower Leg and Ankle

The lower body provides the power and support for a good golf swing. But shinsplints, strained calves, sore Achilles tendons, and unstable ankles can throw the golfers off their games.

✚ SHINSPLINTS

Shinsplints is a wastebasket term used by coaches and some trainers to describe any pain on the inner side of the shin. A true shinsplint is quite rare.

What people call shinsplints are actually pains in the muscles near the shin bone. They can be caused by overuse of the legs, or running and jumping on hard surfaces. They usually occur in people unaccustomed to training, although they can also plague experienced athletes who switch to lighter shoes, harder surfaces, or more concentrated speed work.

The pain is felt on the inner side of the middle third of the shinbone, which is where the muscle responsible for raising the arch of the foot attaches. When the arch collapses with each foot strike, it pulls on the tendon that comes from this muscle.

The arch collapses to absorb the shock of the foot hitting the ground. As you come up on your toes for the next stride, the muscle attached to the arch fires and pulls the arch back up to ready it for the next impact. This muscle responds totally to the stretch of the tendon as the arch flattens.

In people who excessively roll their ankles to the inside (pronate), the arch stays down. Consequently, the muscle starts to fire while there is still weight on the foot, and it is unable to bring the arch up. Because of its multiple firings during each foot strike and its pull against great weight, the arch muscle tears some of its fibers loose from the shinbone. This causes small areas of bleeding around the lining of the bone and pain.

Much more common is the bone stress syndrome. When the ankle rolls over, it rotates the shinbone to the inside. This constant twisting of the bone with each step causes the bone to become sore and painful.

The key element in treatment is an arch support to prevent excessive pronation and pull on the tendon. For beginning pain, propping up the foot with an arch support usually solves the problem almost immediately. For bone stress, it may take 2 to 3 weeks to become pain-free. Most golfers do well with a simple commercial arch support. If you have a more serious problem, you may need an orthotic device custom-made by a sports podiatrist. Icing the sore shin and taking anti-inflammatory medications may also help ease the pain.

MD STRESS FRACTURE

If the twisting of the shinbone is severe and prolonged enough, the bone may become fatigued and crack, just as a piece of metal may do. This is called a stress fracture, and is the last and most disabling of these shin injuries. A stress fracture will need 6 to 8 weeks of rest.

You should suspect a stress fracture if the pain level of bone stress syndrome suddenly increases. Also, if you previously felt pain only while running and you now feel it while walking the course, you may have a stress fracture. See your doctor to confirm your diagnosis with an X ray or a bone scan. If you don't rest a stress fracture, it will only get worse, and the crack in the bone will get larger.

As the fracture heals, treat it with one of the support devices mentioned earlier. If you don't correct your foot strike, you will likely fracture the bone again.

✚ CALF STRAIN

Continuously walking the course can strain calf muscles in the lower leg. The two major muscles of the calf, the gastrocnemius and the soleus, are responsible for lifting the heel and driving you forward as you walk or run.

The simple treatment is to rest for a few days and then begin a gentle, gradual stretching program. Stretch your calf with the Wall Push-Up exercise (page 12). Once the muscle is adequately restretched, re-strengthen it with Toe Raises (page 28).

✚ A SORE ACHILLES

A sore Achilles tendon is a common problem in middle-aged to older golfers. The Achilles tendon, the largest tendon in the body, is found below the calf and helps lift the heel. It may become inflamed and cause tendinitis, or develop a partial tear or rupture completely.

Environmental factors, such as uneven terrain and uphill lies, increase the strain of the tendon. Physical factors are a lack of flexibility and an excessive turning in (pronation) of the foot.

While golfers can not control environmental factors, they can treat physical problems with rest, ice, anti-inflammatory agents, a heel lift, and stretching before and after playing. Physical therapy and an orthotic in the golf shoe may be necessary for resistant cases. If the pain in the Achilles tendon is severe, the golfer should see a doctor to rule out a partial tear or complete rupture, which requires surgery.

✚ ANKLE SPRAINS

An ankle sprain is a fairly uncommon golf injury. When the foot rolls to the outside on an uneven surface, it may continue to roll over until it has stretched and may sprain the not-so-strong ligaments on the outside of the ankle. Large divots and hills on a golf course may lead to mild to moderate ankle sprains.

If you sprain your ankle, you will have swelling and pain in the outer area of the ankle, and you may have black-and-blue marks around the injury. Within a few days, your foot and toes may also be discolored, which comes from blood flowing downward due to gravity.

The best treatment is the RICE formula: Rest, Ice, Compression, and Elevation. Rest your ankle immediately. A sprain's intense pain eases after a few minutes, and you may be tempted to keep playing. But hours later, you may have a sore, swollen, discolored ankle. If you stay off the ankle until the swelling stabilizes, usually you can walk easily within 24 hours.

Ice the ankle until the swelling disappears. The ice curtails bleeding by narrowing blood vessels and helps reduce swelling. Fill a plastic bag with crushed ice and strap it onto the ankle with a towel or elastic bandage. Or you can use a bag of frozen peas or carrots from the supermarket.

Continue icing the ankle for 20 minutes or until it starts to feel numb, and then take off the ice pack and give the ankle enough time to regain some warmth, usually about 20 minutes. Keep icing for 20 minutes on and 20 minutes off for 48 hours or until the ankle returns to normal size.

Compress the ankle in between icings and at night by wrapping it with an elastic bandage, which limits the swelling and bruising.

Elevate the ankle so that it's above your hips and, if possible, above your heart. At night, rest it on pillows or put a suitcase under the mattress at the foot of the bed.

To help reduce stiffness and restore mobility, the golfer can do the following range-of-motion exercise.

Alphabet Range-of-Motion Exercise

Sit in a chair and cross the affected leg over the other leg at the knee. Now, using your big toe as a pointer, trace the capital letters of the alphabet from A to Z. Hold the big toe rigid so all the motion comes from the ankle. Repeat this exercise every hour while you are awake. The letters will be very small at first, but they will increase in size as your range of motion improves.

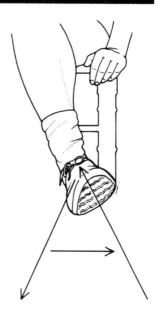

If the sprain is not responding rapidly, do the following exercises to strengthen the ankle.

Ankle Lift

Take a piece of rope about 1.5 feet long, and either tie a 5-pound weight to each end or loop the rope around a 10-pound weight. Sit on a counter and drop the rope over the top of the toes (while wearing an athletic shoe). Lift the weight with your ankle as many times as you can.

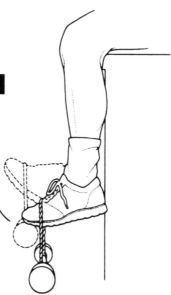

Ankle Turn

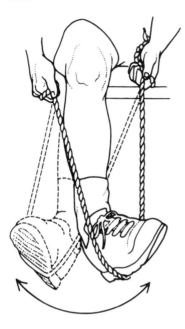

While sitting on a counter, take a long rope, put it under the arch of the shoe of the affected foot, and hold the ends of the rope at about knee height. Turn your ankle as far as it will go to the inside. Now pull on the inside part of the rope and force your ankle to the outside, working against the resistance of the rope. When your foot is all the way out, pull on the outside part of the rope as you bring your foot back to the inside, again working against resistance. Keep the inward and outward movements going until your ankle is fatigued.

Foot Lift (Outward)

While sitting on a counter, hang a weight on your toes, point your foot up, and turn your ankle as far as it will go to the outside. Repeat as many times as you can. Start with a 5-pound weight and work your way up to heavier weights.

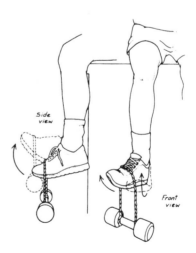

Foot Lift (Inward)

While sitting on a counter, hang a weight on your toes, point your foot up, and turn your ankle as far as it will go toward the inside. Repeat as many times as you can. Start with a 5-pound weight and work your way up to heavier weights.

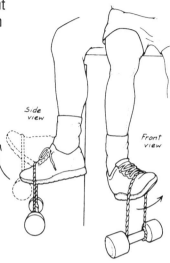

Side view

Front view

Also do the Toe Raise (page 28) and the Heel Drop (page 12), alternating them until your ankle is fatigued. As your ankle gets stronger, lift up your good foot and put all your weight on the injured ankle.

Each of these exercises should be done to the point of total muscle fatigue, so that you can't do even one more.

Balancing is important in retraining an injured ankle to sense where the foot is in relation to the ground. Practice by balancing on one foot with your arms stretched out to the sides until you lose balance or become fatigued. When your ankle gets better, do this exercise with your eyes closed.

The Foot

Good footwork is important in golf, where the feet must roll both to the outside and inside to provide a balanced swing. Various problems from a malaligned foot to high arches to blisters can plague golfers.

While there have been tremendous advances in the design of jogging shoes, basketball sneakers, and hiking shoes, the golf shoe remains basically the same. The only improvement has been the introduction of lighter shoes with soft rubber spikes. There have been no studies of the forces acting on the foot in the golf swing that have translated into an improved shoe. Not only would this reduce foot problems, but it would likely improve golfers' swing dynamics.

✚ FOOT ABNORMALITIES

Structural abnormalities of the foot can cause stress all the way up the leg into the back. The foot may roll to the inside (pronation) or the outside (supination), or the second toe may be longer than the big toe. These problems can be corrected by commercial arch supports, or if foot pain is persistent, orthotic devices that fit inside the golf shoe.

Pronating Foot

The pronating foot has loose ligaments and, because it doesn't have the proper support, rolls to the inside. The foot appears to be flat because the arch becomes compressed when the foot rolls over. But when the weight is taken off the foot, the arch reappears. Someone with true flat feet has no arch at all.

The inward roll of the foot causes the entire leg to rotate to the inside. The kneecaps point toward each other. Everything in the golfer's leg and hip is pulled out of line. The pronating foot causes any number of conditions. These can vary from heel pain and Achilles tendinitis to shin-splints, bone stress syndrome, and stress fracture on the inside of the shinbone to disabling kneecap pain.

A pronating foot can be propped up with an arch support under the inside of the foot. This keeps the foot in line when it strikes the ground and prevents the leg from rolling inward.

Supinating Foot

The supinating, or cavus, foot is the mirror image of the pronating foot. The ligaments are tight, and the foot is rigid with a high arch, which causes the golfer to walk on the far outer portion of the foot. Because the arch is too tight, it cannot collapse when the foot hits the ground. With no arch to absorb the shock of each step, the shock is sent straight up the outside of the leg.

The shock transmission leads to pain on the outer side of the leg. It can cause bone stress syndrome or a stress fracture in the fibula, the small bone on the outside of the shinbone, pain in the outer side of the knee, and even pain extending up into the outer part of the hip.

The supinating foot requires soft padding under the outside of the foot. If you have this problem, I suggest gluing a ¼-inch of soft foam padding from a Dr. Scholl's Flexo Arch along the outside edge of the arch of your golf shoe. This will cause your foot to roll back slightly toward the middle and will provide some padding to reduce the pounding on your leg. Or you may need an orthotic device to take some of the weight off of the outer side of the foot.

Morton's Foot

Morton's foot is characterized by the second toe being longer than the big toe. The problem is that the bone behind the big toe (first metatarsal) is too short. This inherited trait occurs in about 25 percent of the population and causes problems in more people than the other two foot abnormalities combined.

When you walk, you create forward momentum by pushing off with the big toe, which is called toeing off. Just before toeing off, you place all of your weight on the head of the first metatarsal. In golfers with Morton's foot, the first metatarsal is too short to provide the leverage needed to shift the weight to the bottom of the big toe. Instead, the foot buckles to the inside, and the weight rolls along the inner side of the big toe. This is similar to what happens with the pronating foot, but a Morton's foot doesn't pronate until weight is placed on the toes.

Golfers with Morton's foot first strike the ground with the far outer part of the foot. This is probably an unconscious attempt to correct the inward roll of the foot, but it doesn't help prevent the pronation on toeing off. Instead, the golfer ends up walking across the foot, landing on the outside of the heel and then toeing off on the inside of the big toe, instead of walking with a straight-footed, heel-to-toe gait.

Walking on the inner side of the big toe of a Morton's foot usually forms a large callus there. The big toe will also be pushed toward the second toe, and the pressure on the inside of the big toe may cause bunions on the inside of the foot.

Because the Morton's foot starts on the outside of the foot and then pronates at toe-off, it combines the worst features of both the pronating and supinating foot, and can cause all of the conditions they cause.

If you have Morton's foot, you may get by with a commercial arch support along with a foam pad under the big toe. Many commercial arch supports are available for $15 to $40 at drugstores and sporting goods stores.

More likely, you will need an orthotic device that has an arch support and is built up under the big toe joint. Orthotic devices contain carefully placed divots and bumps designed to shift your weight in a way that forces you to walk more naturally. They are made from a variety of materials, from layered foam to leather-covered cork to hard plastic, and can cost several hundred dollars. When your foot starts to buckle, the built-up area in the orthotic will force you to push straight off your foot.

✚ PLANTAR FASCIITIS

Pain in the arch or under the heel while walking is called plantar fasciitis. The plantar fascia is the elastic covering that runs the length of the foot, from just behind the toe bones to the heel bone, that holds up the arch. Overstretching this shock-absorbing layer causes pain and inflammation along the length of the arch.

This injury usually happens to golfers with rigid, high arches. You will feel the pain when pushing off for the next stride or putting weight on the foot. When the arch starts to come down, it stretches the plantar fascia and pulls on its fibers. The torn fibers may go into spasm and shrink. With every step, the plantar fascia tears a little more and causes pain.

The dull pain is particularly bad the first few minutes after rising in the morning or after sitting for a long time. With the weight off of your feet, the plantar fascia will start to heal. But each time you again put weight on your foot, the torn fibers will be pulled apart as the arch collapses.

Treatment consists of supporting the arch with a commercial arch support immediately to prevent the arch from collapsing and the plantar fascia from stretching. Put an arch support in your slippers and wear them as soon as you get out of bed. Even a few steps without support can stretch the plantar fascia. By using arch supports, you will likely feel relief within 2 to 3 days.

Three out of four golfers will do well with an inexpensive commercial arch, while those with a high, rigid arch may need an orthotic for more support.

Plantar fasciitis is particularly common among middle-aged people who have been sedentary and who suddenly increase their level of physical activity. Inappropriately fitting shoes or a weight gain of 10 to 20 pounds can also contribute to the condition.

✚ MORTON'S NEUROMA

Pain, numbness, and sensitivity between the third and fourth toes is known as Morton's neuroma. You may also feel the pain between the second and third toes. Squeezing the forefoot can reproduce the pain, which is caused by pressure on the nerves of the toe bones.

A wider golf shoe may provide relief by easing the pressure. If that does not work, try an orthotic for pressure relief. If that fails, then cortisone injections or surgery may be necessary.

✚ PUMP BUMP

An abnormal, knob-like growth on the back of the heel can be caused by friction and the pressure of the golf shoe's heel counter on the heel bone.

As the weight shifts during the swing, the pressure on the heel bone increases. Not only is this painful, but the Achilles tendon can become inflamed, or the golfer can develop bursitis at that spot.

The treatment includes a heel cup, which holds and cushions the heel within the shoe; padding; a heel counter, to provide cushioning and support; icing the heel bone intermittently; and anti-inflammatory agents for the bursitis pain. Stretching with the Wall Push-Up (page 12) and the Heel Drop (page 12) helps relieve the Achilles tendinitis.

✚ BLISTERS

Blisters form from an improperly fitting golf shoe. New shoes should be broken in by wearing them around the house (preferably on rugs).

To treat a blister, open the top of the blister with a sterilized, sharp instrument, but leave the covering intact. Cover the blister with an antibiotic and a dressing. Blister-prone golfers can use insoles to reduce friction, wear extra cotton or polypropylene socks, lubricate the foot with Vaseline, or apply tape or moleskin to cover pressure points on the foot.

✚ ATHLETE'S FOOT

Golf courses are often wet, particularly from dew early in the morning, and the golfer's shoes and feet can become soaked. Itching and cracking between the toes due to a fungus is called athlete's foot. It can be treated with an antifungal cream or spray available in a drugstore. If athlete's foot persists, see a doctor for a prescription of a stronger antifungal agent.

If you are prone to athlete's foot, make sure the upper of your golf shoe is made of a breathable material, or wear guaranteed waterproof shoes, such as Dry-Joys.

CHOOSING A GOLF SHOE

A golfer's shoes are an essential part of the equipment. Like other areas of golf equipment, golf shoe design has become a high-tech specialty. Dozens of new shoes are introduced each year, from open-toed rubber sandals with spikes to the classic wing tip.

By wearing proper golf shoes, you can reduce the risk of all the injuries that stem from a poor foot strike and lead to pain all the way up the leg to the back.

Newer lightweight golf shoes with supple, contoured uppers, a flexible fit, and plenty of padding underfoot can feel like running shoes with spikes. Look for a structurally sound shoe with a solid, supportive midsole, heavy upper, and lateral reinforcements. Waterproof and breathable linings may make a shoe heavier, stiffer, and more expensive, but they keep your feet dry and allow sweat to get out.

A spikeless shoe no longer means replacing metal spikes with rubber ones. Newer designs use polyurethane spikes or treads dotted with shorter rubber or ceramic nubs, discs, or lateral bars. These spikeless designs minimize wear and tear on greens and offer perfectly good traction for most golfers. Some professionals, including Raymond Floyd and Jack Nicklaus, who have experimented with soft spikes say their feet and legs feel much better, with no sore calves or sore legs, since turning to soft spikes.

Spenco Golf Insoles may also help to cushion your feet and improve your swing balance. The soft rubber insoles, which come in several sizes and can be trimmed to fit your shoe, reduce spike pressure. They are machine-washable and guaranteed for one year.

Part Four

Golf for Everyone

The Senior Game

Women in Golf

The Disabled Golfer

13

The Senior Game

Golfers are different than most athletes: As they grow older, they tend to play more, not less. People over 55 play 50 percent of all rounds and contribute 50 percent to golf revenues every year. As the baby boomer population ages, their sports of choice appear to be golf, tennis, and skiing. While skiing and tennis become less inviting as you get older, golf becomes more attractive.

Golf marketers consider you an avid golfer if you play 25 rounds a year. But when I'm in Florida, I play with older, retired golfers who play 250 rounds a year. This amount of play puts senior golfers at risk for a number of overuse syndromes. The repetitive nature of the golf swing can also exacerbate pre-existing and age-related orthopedic conditions.

Golf has no age limit, and no sport caters as much to the older player. The handicap system allows players to remain competitive as their skills begin to deteriorate. Lighter clubs can be used as your strength declines, and a golf cart as your stamina wanes.

Optimum performance in golf requires strength, flexibility, and endurance, and aging accentuates the loss of these qualities. However, regular exercise and proper nutrition can slow down the loss of physical skills. The effects of aging are more often the result of disuse rather than physical deterioration.

SENIOR CONDITIONING

A properly conceived conditioning program for mature golfers is basically the same as that for younger ones: pre-round warm-up, appropriate

137

stretching, and sport-specific strengthening. While golf is not like running a marathon, endurance is a big part of the game. Without adequate endurance, by the end of a round, the probability of translating difficult shots into successful drives or putts diminishes greatly.

Most seniors take a cart instead of walking the course, but you can get some conditioning by occasionally walking between shots or to the next tee. This will help build up your stamina. To conserve energy, you may need to cut down on the number of balls you hit before a round or limit your practice swings before shots.

Warm-Up

Before playing, the senior golfer should take a brisk walk around the cart area or toward the first tee. If you have time, ride a stationary bicycle for 10 minutes in the locker room or do jumping jacks to raise your body temperature. When you start to break into a sweat, you have warmed up your muscles enough.

Stretching

A stretching program is of the utmost importance for seniors because of declining flexibility. Stretch daily for about 10 to 20 minutes to maintain and increase your flexibility (see chapter 1 for stretching program). Specific attention must be paid to the rotator cuff muscles in the shoulder to improve their length and strength (see chapter 1). Calf muscles are obviously more important for walkers than golf cart riders. The Heel Drop (page 12) helps stretch these lower leg muscles.

Strengthening

Although golf is not a game that requires great strength, a light weight program can prevent loss of strength. Research shows that anyone, even people into their 90s, can gain muscle by doing regular strength training.

The muscles in the stomach and the trunk are responsible for rotating the body and should be worked on daily, if possible. That means doing the Abdominal Crunch (page 25) and the trunk twisting exercises, Bent-Waist Rotation (page 17) and Runners, page 98 in chapter 7. Also do the hip-strengthening exercises on pages 13–15 in chapter 1 and the back-strengthening exercises on pages 97–98 in chapter 7. The Leg Curl (page 26) strengthens the hamstring muscles and the gluteus muscles in the buttocks. The Quadruped Leg Press (page 25) strengthens the hip abductors, which are active during the forward part of the swing. The Thigh Thinner (page 98) also strengthens the trunk.

Special attention must be paid to strengthening the forearm and wrist muscles since seniors tend to lose grip strength. Do Wrist Curls (page 32), Reverse Wrist Curls (page 32), Unbalanced Wrist Rotations (page 32), Roll-Up (page 33), Ball Squeezing (page 33), Arm Curls (page 31), and Reverse Arm Curls (page 31).

Many golfers, especially senior golfers, have neck problems, due to disc or arthritis pain. This can be somewhat prevented by neck-strengthening exercises. You can do basic exercises by applying resistance against yourself or by working with a partner.

Neck-Strengthening Exercises

Neck Tilt Against Resistance

Tilt your head to the right while applying resistance with your right hand, or have a partner apply resistance. Hold for 20 seconds. Then tilt your head to the left and resist with your left hand for 20 seconds. Do the same exercise tilting your head forward and backward.

Shoulder Shrug with Barbell

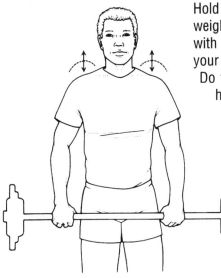

Hold a barbell with 50 pounds of weight straight down in front of you with your elbows locked. Now shrug your shoulders and hold for 5 seconds. Do five repetitions for five sets. This helps build up the trapezius muscles in your neck. If you are starting out, you may need to use less weight and add more gradually. You may even progress past 50 pounds.

SENIORS' INJURIES

Senior golfers need to pay particular attention to overuse injuries because the ability to recover from injuries decreases with age. Hitting bucket after bucket of balls on the practice range can lead to neck or back problems, rotator cuff tendinitis, golfer's elbow, or aggravate other pre-existing injuries.

NECK PAIN

The reason for a high incidence of neck problems among senior golfers is misunderstood. It's not that the senior golfer is rotating his neck more than normal to compensate for stiffness and "taking his eye off the ball." Rather, it comes from the neck position in the swing. The head is held steady and flexed forward ("eyes on the ball") and the body rotates around and under the stationary head. Using a more upright stance and reducing the forward thrust of the head during the swing can reduce discomfort.

Neck pain is best treated conservatively with rest, decreasing your frequency of practice or play during acute pain, and anti-inflammatory medications. A senior golfer may need to decrease the dose of anti-inflammatories because older people tend to have a higher incidence of kidney problems from taking anti-inflammatories over a lifetime. As kidney function decreases with age, the kidneys are less able to excrete anti-inflammatories. In addition, older people are more at risk for gastrointestinal bleeding, particularly women.

A Stretching Program for Pain Relief

To help alleviate minor neck pain, here are some simple exercises. Probably the best neck stretch of them all is the Trapezius Stretch (see page 21, chapter 1). If you have serious neck problems, consult your physician before trying these exercises.

Neck-Stretching Exercises

Chin Drop   *See page 21.*

Funky Pigeon

While sitting down, look slowly to the side, first over one shoulder and then over the other, five times back and forth. Then get "funky" like a pigeon: jut your chin forward and back five times.

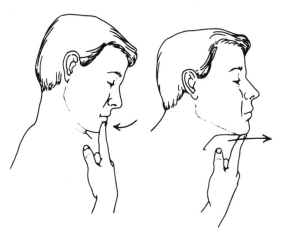

Shoulder Shrug

Lift both shoulders up to your ears and then drop them as low as they can go. Do this five times.

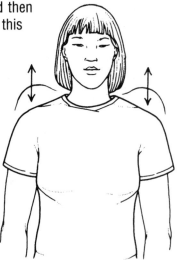

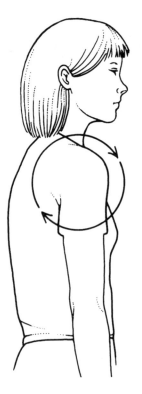

Shoulder Roll

Roll your shoulders by making a circle. Lift both shoulders and roll them forward five times, and then lift and roll them backward five times.

SHOULDER PAIN

Seniors frequently feel shoulder pain from rotator cuff problems. Older golfers may have less blood flow and less space in the shoulder joint due to bony growths that develop over time. The rotator cuff muscles are more brittle and more likely to tear. A specific program of rotator cuff stretching and strengthening is necessary, along with anti-inflammatory medications, if required. Do the Arm Curl (page 31), Reverse Arm Curl (page 31), Front Lift (Palm Down) (page 28), Front Lift (Palm Up) (page 29), Lateral Lift (page 29), Bent-Over Lateral Lift (page 30), and Bent-Over Chest Lift exercises (page 30). If you develop a rotator cuff tear, meticulous surgical repair and exacting rehabilitation are essential for you to be able to return to the game.

The left shoulder of the older right-handed golfer is also at risk for instability. The appropriate treatment is to strengthen the rotator cuff and other shoulder muscles (see above exercises).

LOW-BACK PAIN

Low-back pain is the most frequent complaint among golfers of all ages. The most effective treatment is prevention. Golfers who exercise three or four times a week to strengthen their stomach and trunk muscles are usually able to play without back pain. Do the abdominal and back exercises outlined in chapters 1 and 7. Players on the Senior Professional Golfers Association tour who keep their trunk muscles strong say that they rarely have back pain.

ELBOW PAIN

Sudden impact with the ground when the golfer creates a divot can cause sharp elbow pains. These pains can be treated with rest, ice, and anti-inflammatory agents.

The overuse injury known as golfer's elbow is best treated with rest, stretching, icing, and anti-inflammatory medications, but a limited dose for seniors prone to kidney problems.

Rest does not necessarily mean not playing at all. The senior golfer with elbow problems may switch to the putting green for additional putting and chipping practice until the acute pain subsides.

WRIST PAIN

A golfer of any age may feel wrist pain, frequently in the left wrist, due to overuse. Again, prevention is the best treatment. Attention to proper swing mechanics can reduce the wrist extention during the swing to help resolve this problem.

SEE THE BALL BETTER

Older golfers may have problems seeing the ball. Senior golfers will likely need to wear bifocals, but the lower portion of the bifocal lens is intended for seeing things no more than 18 inches away. So a golf ball on a tee or the ground 3 feet away will look blurry. Squinting to compensate tenses up the shoulders and neck, which affects the golfer's performance.

The best solution is to wear contact lenses for distance vision and reading glasses for close work. Or try reverse bifocals that have tiny reading lenses built into the top part of the eyeglasses. These do not affect distance vision when you look down, and you do not need to switch to reading glasses to mark the scorecard.

A SENIOR STANCE

A better stance can often help the senior golfer. Turning out the big toes of both feet in the setup makes it easier to turn the body in each direction. Stand tall at address to produce a flatter swing, which reduces the stress to the arms and shoulders. Active footwork, lifting the left heel in the backswing and the right heel on the downswing, reduces stress on the hips, knees, and back.

ARTHRITIS

Whether you have played golf for years or are interested in taking up the game at a later age, arthritis does not have to slow you down. Golf can be tailored to meet the physical capabilities of almost anyone. If you have arthritis, playing golf can keep your trunk, hips, and shoulders mobile, plus help you maintain handgrip strength.

Arthritis patients need to modify their equipment to fit their medical condition. Grips, shoes, balls, and clubs can all be adapted to fit your needs and abilities. Your local pro shop or golf specialty store can help you select products to make golfing easier on your joints. The Arthritis Foundation recommends the following guidelines:

- Use a lower compression ball—for example, 90 compression instead of 100—which feels softer because it gives more when you hit it.
- Use clubs with lightweight graphite shafts to help absorb shock better.
- Use perimeter-weighted clubs for better shock absorption, particularly from off-center hits.
- Build up the grip size on your clubs with epoxy tape to help you hold them easier and to reduce stress and pain on your finger joints.
- Try wearing wrist braces and gloves on both hands to stabilize your joints.
- Wear comfortable walking shoes or spikeless golf shoes.

To compensate for wrist or hand arthritis, a senior golfer can place the left thumb around, rather than on top of, the shaft to allow for freer wrist movement. Also, minimize hand and wrist movement in your pitch shots to lessen discomfort caused by sore joints. Handsy pitches can result in a more jarring impact.

A good conditioning program is essential for all golfers, but especially if your joints need extra protection. Proper conditioning helps maintain range of motion in the joints and reduces your chances of injury.

When you take lessons, don't be afraid to explain your physical limitations to your instructor. If you don't have a golf instructor, your local golf shop should be able to recommend someone who assists anyone with physical limitations.

Once you are on the links, there are other adaptations that can make the game more enjoyable and safer for your joints. The Arthritis Foundation recommends that you keep these suggestions in mind:

- Always loosen up beforehand with a few minutes of walking. Spend 5 to 10 minutes stretching, then take 10 to 15 hits off the practice range before heading for the first tee. Easy practice swings, trunk twists, hamstring stretches, and walking are good warm-up exercises.

- Use tees whenever you hit the ball, even on the practice range, to avoid striking the ground and jarring your joints.

- Keep your grip tension on the shaft consistent to add consistency to your swing and heighten your overall comfort.

- If you have back pain, you may find that the Classic swing with an upright follow-through is more comfortable than the Modern swing with a reverse-C follow-through.

- Always brush through the grass so you will hit the ball solidly and carry your momentum out to the target.

- Play from 150-yard markers if you begin to get tired.

- Consider using energy-saving techniques while you are on the course. Pull your golf bag instead of carrying it, or rent a motorized cart instead of walking.

- Remember that it's okay to play less than a full 18-hole round. Look for a nearby 9-hole course or check into playing a 9-hole round at your local course. Many courses now offer 9-hole leagues as well.

- Listen to your body throughout the round. If you begin to tire, practice your chipping or putting, or play fewer holes.

14

Women in Golf

A subtle change has taken place over the past few years in golf. More women are whacking golf balls on the range or practicing on the putting green. Large displays of women's golf equipment and apparel seems to have appeared overnight in golf pro shops. And women professionals now get nearly equal coverage in the media with their male counterparts.

These are all signs of the continuing growth in women's golf. While only one in five of today's golfers are women, women make up nearly 40 percent of new golfers. Junior girls are the fastest-growing group of golfers. Hard on their heels are women executives who are using their well-honed organizational skills to found leagues of their own.

With a need for a sense of ownership and places to play, several executive women's golf leagues have sprung up across the country. As a group, executive women are growing exponentially, armed with financial clout and a strong desire to learn and master the game quickly. In just three years, the Executive Women's Golf League has gone from 28 members to more than 7,000 in 75 chapters nationwide. The average member is 43 years old, earns a personal salary of $62,700, and has a husband who earns at least as much, if not more. She obviously has discretionary income to spend, and wants to spend it on golf.

There may not be as many women golfers as men, but what women lack in numbers they make up in purchasing power. According to the National Golf Foundation, infrequent women golfers spend four times as much as their male counterparts on lessons, videos, and magazines.

Frequent women golfers play more, travel more, and spend more than their male counterparts. Women make more than 85 percent of all golf apparel purchases.

The women golfers I know are not as competitive on the golf course as men. They are not as driven by ego to try to prove that they are better than their peers, as men tend to be. Women seem more concerned about the rules and not as much about gambling. They seem to enjoy the game of golf more than men, and I admire them for that.

To be at the top of their games, women golfers need to improve their strength, particularly upper-body strength, and to work on stretching, posture, and balance, some of which they can do at home or at work.

GAINING STRENGTH

Women can approximate the strength of men in the lower body, but not the upper body, where men have a genetic advantage. The human male has an innate potential to develop bigger shoulders, chest, and arms than the human female. According to medical studies, a woman has roughly two-thirds the muscle mass of a comparably sized man. Although most of the power of the golf swing comes from the legs and hips, which are strong in women, the lack of upper body strength requires a lighter club, and this decreases the impact a woman can apply to the ball.

Women should buy clubs that are specifically engineered for them. For years, women's equipment was a version of men's painted a bright color, which means women were playing with clubs that were too heavy for them. Women generally need a more flexible shaft to compensate for less upper-body strength. They need clubs that allow them to drive a long way, get their fairway woods in the air, and hit their long irons straight. New high-performance equipment engineered specifically for women is now available. The current trend is for high-tech, high-end equipment, and manufacturers are extending their lines knowing that serious women golfers are willing to pay for top performance.

Women should use the same swing as men, which means using the big muscles. Anyone can gain distance by restricting the hip turn and coiling more with the upper body. A complete upper-body and shoulder turn, coupled with a restricted hip and lower-body turn, stores energy.

In an attempt to generate extra power, many women try to hit the ball with their hands. They throw themselves out of balance, spin forward out of the shot, and fall back on their right leg. By hitting hard at the ball, all a woman does is accelerate the butt of the club, not the head. A smooth swing using more of the lower body will hit the ball farther. Luckily, women golfers tend to be more supple than men on the whole, especially in the hips. This makes them particularly well equipped to execute a fluent swing with a longer arc to generate clubhead speed.

A weight-training program can tighten and strengthen golf-related and other muscles. Through weight training, women can increase their upper-body strength markedly without bulking up as men do. This is because women have little circulating male hormone, which is required for bulking up. The huge upper bodies you see on female weight trainers are due to steroid use. As long as a female golfer has a normal level of circulating female hormones and doesn't take any artificial male hormones, she will increase her strength and not her bulk through weight training.

BONE STRENGTH

Bone strength is important for women, particularly as they age. A menstrual disturbance in a young female athlete can increase her risk of bone loss and stress fractures. Amenorrhea, the lack of a menstrual period, in a young athlete usually leads to insufficient bone mineral density. With aging, she will lose bone tissue and be vulnerable to the bone-wasting disease of osteoporosis.

Osteoporosis is the thinning of the bones due to loss of bone mass. The bones of the skeleton become porous, brittle, and more easily breakable in women and men with osteoporosis. During childhood and early adult life, more bone is made than is broken down. However, by age 35, there is a net loss of bone, which is accelerated around age 65. Osteoporosis affects 25 percent of American women and it may be severe, resulting in crippling and disfigurement. It has been estimated that 1.3 million women per year will have bone fractures because of underlying osteoporosis.

The preponderance of osteoporosis in women is believed to be related to sudden decreases in estrogen levels in their bodies. Estrogen is vital to proper bone growth because it allows calcium to be absorbed from the intestines, and calcium is a necessary ingredient in building the skeleton.

Osteoporosis may become a factor in golfers due to stress on the spine. Older women should avoid the reverse-C follow-through and use the Classic swing instead. A good weight-training program helps to slow the development and degree of osteoporosis. Both estrogen and calcium supplements can help optimize bone mass, although estrogen therapy is controversial. See your doctor for an individual assessment of your risk.

Preventing Osteoporosis

There are several factors that may prevent the development of osteo-porosis. The first is to take an adequate amount of calcium in the diet throughout life so that bones are built up before bone loss begins at age 35. Estrogen therapy can sometimes be successful, and exercise is bene-ficial by strengthening the bones.

Diet is extremely important in preventing osteoporosis, and calcium-rich dairy products should be included in the diet. These foods tend to be high in calories and cholesterol, so choose low-fat versions whenever possible. In addition, excessive calcium loss may occur from soft drinks, coffee and alcohol, and nicotine in cigarettes, so limit your intake of these beverages and, of course, try to cut down or stop smoking.

The recommended daily allowance of calcium is 1 gm (1,000 mg) for women over age 19 and 1.2 to 1.5 gm (1,200 to 1,500 mg) for women after menopause to avoid osteoporosis. To take in this amount of calcium usually requires calcium supplements, since the average American diet contains about 600 or 700 mg of calcium. If you are consider-ing calcium supplements, check with your physician for the right kind for you.

Several new drugs have won approval from the Food and Drug Ad-ministration (FDA) to prevent osteoporosis and fractures in post-menopausal women with osteoporosis, one of the few instances drugs have been indicated to prevent a chronic disease. These new drugs, known as bisphosphonates, including alendronate and etidronate, pro-vide a nonhormonal option for preventing rapid bone loss in the early postmenopausal period, the bone loss that may lead to osteoporosis and fractures.

Weight-bearing exercises, such as walking, dancing, and jogging, are particularly valuable in reducing bone loss in middle-aged and postmenopausal women. I recommend that all female golfers get regular, weight-bearing exercise to help prevent osteoporosis. This includes taking a 4- to 5-mile walk while playing a typical 18-hole round. In fact, a recent study of female caddies found that they had significantly denser bones and stronger muscles than nongolfers of the same age.

Confusing Osteoporosis with Osteoarthritis

New research suggests that confusion surrounding osteoporosis and osteoarthritis is so extensive that many women may be waiting for the swollen joints, stiffness, and pain typically associated with arthritis to occur before they become concerned about osteoporosis. Since osteoporosis is a symptomless, painless disease until a fracture occurs, the National Osteoporosis Foundation (NOF) has issued an advisory that warns women against waiting for symptoms to develop before seeking a diagnosis or discussing their risk for osteoporosis with their doctors.

The Public Health Advisory suggests that in addition to educating themselves about osteoporosis and assessing personal risk with their doctors, women also should ask their physicians about the need for a bone density measurement test, using special X-ray machines, to assess the state of the bones and potential risk for future fractures. Although highly accurate in predicting fracture risk, bone density measurements are underutilized, perhaps because women may be waiting for symptoms before taking the risk of osteoporosis seriously.

The FDA recently approved the first osteoporosis test that does not use X rays, which may prove to be easy, portable, and inexpensive, and reach women who have had no access to bone testing. The new device uses ultrasound, or high-frequency sound waves, to assess a woman's bones by measuring the density of her heel. You slip your foot into a small box about the size of a laser printer, and the sound waves painlessly penetrate for 10 seconds. Bone density is determined by how easily and quickly the sound waves move. The machine automatically analyzes the results within minutes. Each test costs about $40, much less than about $125 for the leading X-ray test.

A low test score does not necessarily mean you have osteoporosis. Your doctor must also assess other risks, including a family history of hip fracture or if you are small-framed, light-skinned, or a cigarette smoker.

A survey of more than 500 American women found that 6 women in 10 think that osteoporosis has warning signs or symptoms when, in fact, the disease progresses without signs or symptoms until a fracture occurs. Of those surveyed, 71 percent cited pain, half mentioned stiffness, and one-third referred to swollen joints as symptoms of osteoporosis, but those are actually symptoms of arthritis.

In addition, half of the women surveyed indicated that they believe there are similar treatment approaches for arthritis and osteoporosis, although the treatments are vastly different. In fact, in some cases the treatment for one of these diseases may cause or worsen the other. For example, a common drug used for treating one form of arthritis is corticosteroids, which can lead to osteoporosis when used in high doses for long periods of time. At the same time, a program of regular, weight-bearing exercises, which are highly beneficial for preventing osteoporosis and maintaining strong bones, may worsen the condition of joints affected by osteoarthritis.

STRETCHING

Stretching before a round can reduce the likelihood of soreness afterward. Women need to pay close attention to stretching the calf muscles, which may already be shortened from wearing shoes with higher heels off the course. Do the Heel Drop (see page 12) every day if you can, and certainly before going out to play.

For other muscles, do the following stretches:

To loosen your trunk muscles, do the Side Stretch. See page 17.

To stretch your hamstring and buttock muscles, do the Hurdler Stretch (Standing). See page 11.

To stretch you shoulder muscles, follow the shoulder stretching program outlined in chapter 6.

POSTURE AND BALANCE

One of the worst golf problems women face is bad posture and poor balance. For example, if you have weak abdominal muscles, you tend to lean over too much when addressing the ball, which can add 25 percent more strain on your back. Good weight distribution is the foundation of balance and relieves tension.

You can develop better balance with a few simple exercises. Practice standing on one foot with your arms stretched out to the sides until you lose balance or become fatigued. Repeat with the other foot. Once you can do this easily, do it with your eyes closed, which is more difficult.

Proper weight shift preserves balance throughout the swing. In front of a mirror, fold your arms and place your hands on opposite shoulders with your back bent slightly. Turn your shoulders to the right so that all of your weight rests on the right foot. Lift the left heel and turn your shoulders to the left. You should feel your weight shifting back to the left side. When you finish, your weight transfer should be complete and the right heel should be up.

For more balance training, you can stand on a balancing board, which is a board that rests on a cylinder and allows you to roll back and forth, or a BAPS board, which is a round platform that balances on half a ball. Ask a personal trainer or physical trainer to help you learn how to use a balancing board correctly. You can also improve your balance with the big rubber ball described in chapter 5 (page 75). Again, have someone who has experience with these balls set up a program for you.

PROBLEM AREAS

A woman golfer's injuries are basically the same as a man's. But there are some peculiarities due to differences in anatomy.

Hand Strength

Male professional golfers may have better short games than female professionals because they have stronger hands. Women need better hand strength to make the small movements that are essential to a great short game. Many women are unable to support the weight of the club at the top of the swing due to lack of hand and wrist strength. To improve your strength, do the hand and wrist strengthening and stretching exercises outlined in chapters 1 and 9.

Also, make sure that your grip size is correct. A grip that's too small or too large forces you to hold the club too tightly. This can lead to fatigue in hand and forearm muscles and places additional stress on elbow tendons.

Knee Pain

Women are more at risk to develop runner's knee than men. This is because they have a wider pelvis, making the angle between the thigh and the calf sharper. This increases the tendency for the kneecap to pull out of line and rub on the side of its groove, causing knee pain. Women should be more aware of early signs of knee pain. Orthotic devices worn in golf shoes and other shoes can correct for runner's knee and relieve the pain. The 30-Degree Leg Extension, not the full leg extension, outlined on page 119 in chapter 10 can also help by strengthening the quadriceps muscle.

Breast Size

Increased breast size may limit how far a woman's arms can cross the chest. But large breasts should not limit your backswing. If you feel your breasts are interfering with your swing, see a professional instructor to make any necessary corrections.

Today's sports bras now provide much-needed breast support. All of the different shapes and sizes of sports bras are designed to minimize breast motion. They press the breasts against the chest, and they cradle and restrain each breast separately within a cup. A good sports bra is sturdy but not constricting and allows a full range of motion. Most are made of nonabrasive, breathable materials.

Since there are so many sports bras available, evaluate each one before you make a purchase. When trying on a bra, run in place, do some jumping jacks, and take some mock practice swings. You want to make sure you get all the support you need.

For less impact-driven sports such as golf, look for ventilation in cleavage and underarm areas. Some sports bras now have breathable, wicking materials that dry quickly. Once you're done playing, simply rinse the bra in a sink and set it out to dry. Then it will be ready to use within a few hours, a great advantage if you're on a golf trip and plan to play frequently.

Pregnancy

Most women can continue to play golf while pregnant. A pregnant women simply needs to consult her doctor, follow some simple guidelines, and pay attention to her body for signs of fatigue.

The pregnant golfer should drink lots of water, especially when it's hot, and take plenty of snacks on the course. Walk the course, but have someone in your group take a cart in case you get tired. Make sure to use a restroom before playing and at the turn, if not more often.

Around the sixth month of pregnancy, you may need to make some adjustments in your golf game. By that time, your hands and feet may be swollen. Try a larger glove and a pair of stretched-out golf shoes. If you have trouble addressing the ball comfortably, bend a little more at the hips or step back from the ball a few inches. This should permit your arms to hang freely from the shoulders. To accommodate for a bigger belly and breasts, try to achieve a balanced swing with an even pace.

Keeping fit and maintaining good muscle tone is an important part of health care during pregnancy. Exercise prepares the body for labor, promotes good bowel function, aids in sleep, and makes a woman feel better in general. Women who exercise regularly during pregnancy have fewer cesarean births, less pain during delivery, shorter hospital stays, and slightly heavier babies compared to nonexercising women.

Strengthening muscles will help a woman deal with the low-back pain and other problems encountered during pregnancy due to weight gain and an altered center of gravity. There is no reason for a pregnant woman to avoid lifting heavy objects, such as a golf bag. That old myth should be put to rest.

Women who are in a regular exercise program certainly shouldn't take 9 months off from golf. If you are planning a pregnancy, you should exercise to get in shape before you become pregnant and then maintain your fitness during pregnancy.

Most prenatal classes, in addition to offering a selection of aerobically based exercises, have mothers-to-be work on specific muscle groups. These include three major areas that all female golfers should emphasize: the shoulders and back, the abdominals, and the muscles at the base of the pelvis.

The safest sports during pregnancy are those that offer smooth, continuous activity as well as conditioning. Golf, walking, swimming, cross-country skiing, and cycling are all excellent.

AT-WORK AND HOME EXERCISES

Women, as well as men, can put in daily workouts when they do not have the time to practice. You can incorporate these at-work or home exercises into the day to improve flexibility and strength. These exercises focus on the upper body, where women need particular assistance, and the back, a problem area for every golfer.

Shoulder Flexibility

Increased flexibility increases the range of motion in the swing. While in the car or at work, place both hands on the steering wheel or a desk and roll your shoulders forward in a clockwise direction, then again in a counterclockwise direction, 10 times in each direction. Then shrug the shoulders upward. Hold for 3 seconds, and release. Repeat 10 times.

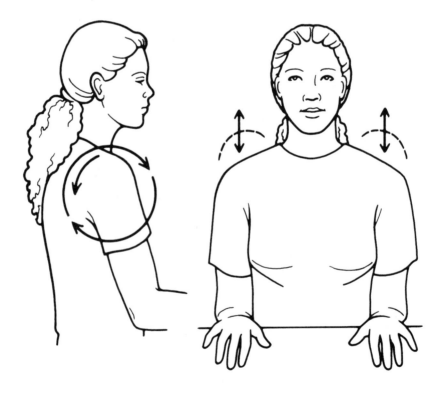

Wrist Cock

Strong wrists lead to a sound grip. Take a break while at work and hold your hands as if gripping a club. Raise them to waist height and cock your hands upward toward the right shoulder. Return your hands to waist height and cock them toward the left shoulder. Keep your elbows near the ribs throughout. Repeat 30 times.

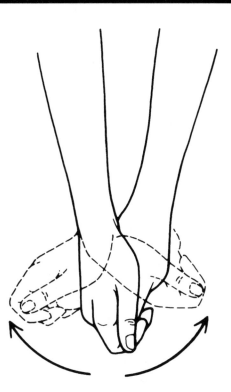

Lower Back Flexibility

A flexible lower back increases strength and decreases the likelihood of injuries. While watching television, sit in a chair with your back flat against the back of the chair and with a club lying across your shoulders. Slowly turn the upper body to the right, keeping the hips as quiet as possible, but not rigid. Hold the stretch for 10 to 20 seconds. Then rotate slowly to the left and hold again for 10 to 20 seconds. Do not simply rotate back and forth, which only causes muscles to fire and shorten, not lengthen.

Rotator Cuff Strength

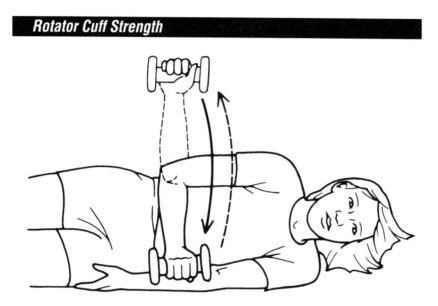

Building up rotator cuff muscles prevents this common shoulder injury. This exercise will help allow the arm to rotate back in the swing and then get the club going forward. While watching television, lie on your right side with your back to a couch. Place your right hand on your right hip. Hold a small (2- to 3-pound) hand weight in your left hand, with the left elbow touching the left hip and the weight directly over the hip. Drop your left forearm forward toward the television and across the chest, then raise your forearm back over your hip. Keep your left elbow close to the left hip during the entire movement. Do three sets of 10 repetitions. Switch sides and work your right arm through the same exercise.

The Disabled Golfer

Golf is a sport that is available to a wide variety of disabled people. You can ride a cart if you can't walk long distances, and your swing can be adapted to get around many disabilities.

The United States Golf Association (800-336-4446), in its *Rules of Golf,* has a section on golfers with disabilities, including golfers who use wheelchairs, crutches, and canes, and those who have lost a limb or their vision.

LEG PROBLEMS

Casey Martin's leg problems and his dispute with the PGA over the use of a golf cart has brought more disabled golfers out of the closet and onto the course. Martin won the right in court to ride a cart during professional tournaments, which he has done while playing in the minor-league Nike tour and in some PGA Tour events.

Martin suffers from a rare, hereditary circulatory disorder. His lower right leg has been a source of pain since birth. The primary vein in his right leg is missing, and smaller veins are malformed. Because blood moves slowly, his leg is malnourished and smaller than normal size. When he stands, blood does not rise from his lower leg. Blood becomes trapped in his veins and his leg turns dark red, even black looking.

His degenerative disease (Klippel-Trenaunay-Weber syndrome) causes him to wake frequently during the night with leg pain. While he says his leg feels better riding than walking, his condition is progressing. He is at serious risk of a fracture, and he will eventually lose the leg and need a prosthesis to continue playing. His orthopedist designed a device extending from his toes to mid-calf to protect and support the leg bones, but Martin couldn't play very well with it.

Many more people develop circulatory disturbances as they age. They can have intermittent claudication, which is leg cramps due to an insufficient blood supply. These golfers will begin to get leg cramps after walking a few minutes. Sitting and resting is the only way to get relief. Anyone with a circulatory problem, or those with neurological or muscle-wasting diseases such as polio, can ride a cart around the course.

AMPUTEES

Many amputees play golf well. Some of these golfers can even walk the whole course, but, of course, they can ride if this is beyond their capacity. Newer prostheses are much more sophisticated and can closely approximate normal movement and function.

Golfers who have lost an arm or the function of an arm can learn to swing one-handed. While this will cut down on distance and somewhat on accuracy, these golfers are not precluded from the sport, as they would be in most other sports.

JOINT REPLACEMENT

Arthritis can cause joints to deteriorate to the point where they need replacing. But there is no reason for a joint replacement to prevent a full return to golf. Even people who have two artificial hip prostheses can continue to play. Surveys show that the average time to playing golf is 3 to 4 months after a hip replacement, with some golfers returning as early as 1 month. (Now golf legend Jack Nicklaus is talking about the possibility of having a hip replacement.) A total knee replacement or shoulder replacement should not preclude a return to golf, although most orthopedic surgeons highly recommend that a golfer with an artificial knee use a motorized golf cart.

Here are some tips for post-prosthesis players:

- Avoid playing in wet weather. Many golfers with artificial hip or knee joints play better without spikes because their feet can turn and take some pressure off the artificial joints. However, your chances of slipping and falling is slightly increased in wet weather without metal spikes.

- Play "on your toes." On the backswing, lift the left heel, and on the downswing lift the right heel. This helps ease the pressure on artificial joints, while swinging flatfooted increases the pressure.

Right-handed players with right knee replacements may benefit from the "stepping through" technique popularized by Senior PGA professional Gary Player: the right leg comes off the ground on the downswing and follows through as the golfer steps toward the target. Never attempt this if you have a left knee prosthesis because it will overload the joint.

A right-handed golfer with a left knee replacement may benefit from an open stance facing the target. This makes the back swing more difficult, but raising the left knee allows for an adequate back swing.

PARAPLEGICS

Another shining example of a disabled golfer is Dennis Walters, a golf professional without the use of his legs. A promising amateur golfer in his youth, Walters had a golf cart accident and became a paraplegic. He was told he would never play golf again. But he never lost his love for the game, and he constructed a seat that swings out of the side of a golf cart. From this swiveling seat, he can hit balls, and he has learned how to maneuver with crutches to play out of bunkers and to putt. He is now part of the traveling trick-shot show, mixing inspiration and entertainment in his stops around the country. Walters still enjoys golf and comradeship on the course, as can other paraplegic golfers with a little ingenuity.

BAD BACK

The golfer with a bad back may be able to continue to play by modifying the swing. Going from the Modern reverse-C swing to the Classic straight-back swing, as described on page 92, may allow continued participation, especially if combined with a back-strengthening program (see page 97).

Index